FRANCIS BACON

FRANCIS BACON

By A. R. SKEMP, M.A., Ph.D.

KENNIKAT PRESS
Port Washington, N. Y./London

FRANCIS BACON

First published in 1912
Reissued in 1970 by Kennikat Press
Library of Congress Catalog Card No: 77-103212
SBN 8046-0849-0

Manufactured by Taylor Publishing Company   Dallas, Texas

CONTENTS

FRANCIS BACON

CHAPTER I

THE DAYS OF PREPARATION

THE life of Francis Bacon (1561–1626) covers the period
of richest fulfilment in England of the Renascence spirit.
Within the decade before his birth had been born
Spenser, the poet who best expresses the positive moral
and æsthetic ideals of the English Renascence ; Hooker,
whose fine spirit apprehended the best elements in the
settlement of the English Church, and whose massive
intellect took service under his intense religious instinct
to give a defined position, a coherent justification, and
a philosophical apology to that wise compromise between
inherited faith, reforming zeal, and political exigency ;
and Sidney, poet and soldier, lover and philosopher,
idealist and courtier, the very perfect gentle knight of
the new chivalry. Two years after him were born
Marlowe, in whose wild genius blazed into expression
the Renascence craving for utter emotional and intellectual freedom and fulfilment ; and Shakespeare, in
whom the fire of the new youth of the world brightened
into the clearest flame of supreme genius.

In this galaxy Bacon shines with the " dry light "
which he praised for the illumination of truth ; a cold
star, lighting the way of intellectual progress. Among
the Elizabethans, Bacon stands second in intellectual
power only to Shakespeare. His devotion to knowledge, his sense that he was " born to serve mankind,"
his optimism concerning man's ultimate government of

7

Nature, the independence and vastness and massive
power of his intellect, his foresight and insight as a
statesman, the strength and beauty of his style, now
terse and epigrammatic, now dignified and flowing,
always lucid and vivid—all these compel admiration.
But no man of comparable greatness offers less attrac-
tion to hero-worship. This is not merely because some
of Bacon's actions stand open to grave criticism, not
because an extreme judgment might condemn him as
non-moral or immoral. The gulf between Bacon's
intellectual position and the usual moral-sentimental
Victorian position was indeed too great to be bridged ;
but a generation trained in criticism of traditional moral
standards by Nietzsche, or at least by Mr. Bernard
Shaw, should understand Bacon's character better
and judge his actions more tolerantly than did most
nineteenth century critics. Comprehension, however,
brings no feeling warmer than admiration and pity,
for Bacon himself stood aloof from warmer emotions.
He used love and friendship, and hate and fear, and
all personal emotions, as tools of the cold, governing
mind. Personal ambition he knew, and the nobler
ambitions of the scientist and statesman ; patriotism
he felt, and the wider emotion that seeks the progress
of all mankind ; he was jealous of his rivals, he
despised the little minds that baffled him, he was
moderately grateful to those who helped him ; but he
was never the servant of either the best or the worst
of these feelings. He cherished great ideals and served
them devotedly, but he never sacrificed himself for
them.

But though Bacon's life thus fails to make the intimate
personal appeal of the life of Sidney or Raleigh, it is
fascinating in its perfectly coherent revelation of a most
striking personality, and its climax moves the dramatic
imagination. It is impossible to follow this story of a
great character betrayed by its own weakness to the
attack of circumstance, without feeling its tragedy, and
paying due tribute of pity and awe.

Bacon was marked out for great opportunities by his

birth. His father, Sir Nicholas Bacon, was Lord Keeper
of the Great Seal. His mother was a daughter of Sir
Anthony Cook, tutor of Edward VI. Her sister married
Sir William Cecil, who became Lord Burghley in 1571
and Lord Treasurer in 1572. Francis was born on
January 22nd, 1561, at York House, in the Strand,
the Lord Keeper's official residence; a house later to be
the object of poignant associations, for Bacon became
its master as Lord Chancellor in the hour of his triumph,
and yielded it as the price of Buckingham's protection
in the hour of his fall. His childhood was spent partly
at York House, partly at his father's country house at
Gorhambury, in Hertfordshire. He was the youngest
of eight children—six by his father's first marriage,
and one full brother, Anthony, with whom he was particularly closely associated during the later years of his
boyhood.

Sir Nicholas Bacon was a sound lawyer, an honest,
independent and intelligent statesman, a warm friend
to education. Puttenham, North and Ben Jonson
attest his eloquence, and a wealth of contemporary
evidence proves the wide popularity which he gained
by his genial temper and his pleasant wit. Bacon's
character owed more, however, to his mother than to
his father. It is reported that Lady Ann Bacon assisted
her father in instructing Edward VI.; certainly she
was one of the learned women of the day, mistress of
Latin, Greek, Italian and French. More noteworthy
even than her scholarship was her fervent and un-
wavering zeal for Puritanism. She used her learning
and her influence alike in its service, and her extant
letters to her sons, at Cambridge and at Gray's Inn,
show how strenuously she endeavoured to impart to
them her own Puritan zeal. Sir Nicholas also showed
Puritan leanings, though his chief desire was to establish the Church of England firmly. Bacon thus grew
up in an atmosphere which prepared him to feel tolerantly towards the Puritans; and the width of view
and wisdom of judgment which mark his writings on
Church controversies may be traced in some part to his

early training. The massive practical sense of Bacon safeguarded him from following his mother in her wilder flights ; indeed fanaticism of all kinds repelled him, and without the influence of his early training he might well have failed in justice to the Puritans. His temperament made him moderate, his training helped to make him tolerant, and he extended to the Catholics the fairness of judgment which he had first learned for the sake of their bitterest enemies.

The earliest influences in Bacon's life were thus high and serious. The child would perhaps appreciate rather the dignity and power of his father's office than the greatness of the affairs concerned ; but at least he would learn to think familiarly of great persons and movements. He would feel above all the supreme power of the Queen, and as he grew older he may well have heard something of the care and diplomacy needed in working for her. He commenced courtier while still a boy ; the Queen asked his age, and he answered : " Only two years younger than your Majesty's happy reign." The answer, with its apt emphasis on the memorable fact under which the little personal fact must fall, suited the grave, self-possessed yet deferential boy, and pleased the Queen ; and she named him " her young Lord Keeper."

Of his early education we know little. Early in his thirteenth year, in April 1573, he and his brother Anthony were sent up to Trinity College, Cambridge, where Whitgift, later Archbishop of Canterbury, was their tutor. Whitgift's influence, thrown wholly on the side of the Established Church, doubtless strengthened Bacon's natural inclination to the most practical solution of the religious controversies. Scant record remains of these undergraduate days. We learn, from charges paid to the " potigarie," that both boys were rather sickly ; and both gained a reputation for assiduous study. According to a late reminiscence of Bacon's, recorded by his first biographer (his chaplain, Dr. Rawley), he began, even in these days to distrust Aristotle, not for his matter, but for " the unfruitfulness of his way." The

academic tradition of the Middle Ages still lingered in
England, and Aristotle was the idol of its worship.
Bacon was constitutionally incapable of idol-worship—
a characteristic that explains some of his limitations as
well as much of his greatness. His vigorous and sinewy
mind was ever ready to wrestle for the blessing of truth ;
and it may well be that even in these early days he
tried a fall with the greatest of the established champions
of philosophy.

In June 1576 the two brothers were admitted together
to Gray's Inn as " ancients " (*de societate magistrorum*).
Finally, completing his education in the recognized
way, Francis was sent abroad to widen his experience
and gain an insight into diplomatic methods. He
was attached to the household of Sir Amyas Paulet,
who went to France in September 1576, and took up
duty as ambassador in the following February. Bacon
spent the next two years with the embassy, following
the Court from Paris to Blois, to Tours, to Poitiers.
These years held many stirring events—the intrigues
of Don John of Austria with Mary Queen of Scots,
planning their marriage and the invasion of England ;
a Portuguese plan for the invasion of Ireland, supported
by Spain and the Pope ; civil war in France—events
offering education of a different kind from that of the
University and Gray's Inn. We can imagine Bacon's
patriotism and loyalty growing more devoted in face of
attacks on his country and his Queen ; his Protestantism
growing more definitely political, and more careless of
theological issues, in face of political Catholicism ; his
sense of the evil of civil war quickening by observation ; and his mind developing among new experiences,
testing its ideals and theories by practical life and
learning the supple and cynical wisdom of political
intrigue.

Bacon's apprenticeship to diplomacy was brought to
an abrupt and sad close. In February 1579 his father
died, very suddenly, from the effects of a chill. Bacon
recorded later, in *Sylva Sylvarum*, that a dream warned
him before the news arrived ; he dreamt that his father's

house in the country was plastered all over with black mortar. The circumstance is noteworthy, for such an experience, whatever its explanation, must have disposed Bacon to view the so-called supernatural with more credulity. The suddenness of Sir Nicholas Bacon's death was calamitous to Bacon's material prospects. After providing for his other sons, his father had set aside a large sum to purchase an estate for Francis. Death prevented the provision, and Francis inherited only one-fifth of the fortune devised for him. His prospects were completely changed. The son of the great minister, with independent means, might have chosen his career freely ; fatherless, confronted by the need of making a living suitable to his position, with no more powerful support than the uncertain friendship of an uncle by marriage, he had no choice. His training, the example of his father's career, the hope that the influence he might expect to command would here be especially serviceable, the substantial prizes to be gained, the suitability of the profession as preparation for more attractive offices of state, all pointed to the law; and Bacon at once turned to the law as the immediate practical business of his life.

For a man of stronger character, this change of prospect might have been actually beneficial. The sense of self-dependence might have spurred him on to effort without any sacrifice of lofty purpose or of freedom of personality. But Bacon's moral constitution was not strong enough to bear the harsh discipline of adversity. The longing for power and for variety of experience, so characteristic of the Renascence, was strong in Bacon. In one mood he believed that he was " more fitted to hold a book than to govern affairs " ; but the scholar's life could not in any circumstances have satisfied him. The ultimate aim of his philosophy was to govern Nature ; and the governing temper, fostered by a boyhood passed among statesmen, could not turn away from practical affairs. " Only the dull are modest," and Bacon knew his own powers. He wished to use them in the service of his country and of mankind, but he wanted more than the mere joy of service. His desire not only for power, but also for the pomp and circumstance of power, was instinctive and unappeasable ; and it sometimes drove him along devious paths. Intellectually he towers above his age ; in moral sense he is an average Elizabethan, keener indeed in apprehending the intellectual element in morality, correspondingly more contemptuous of the useful, unreflecting traditions of honourable action. He was adventurer and patriot, scholar and man of affairs, egoist and altruist. Endowed with true political wisdom, and eager to serve his country well, his desire to keep his sovereign's favour could make him believe that the best way to his great end was the crooked way of flattery and timeserving compromise. Hungry for the truth, and nobly confident in the power of knowledge, he could yet subordinate his pursuit of knowledge to his pursuit of place. Zealous to serve mankind, he was not prepared in that service to imperil the immediate interests of Francis Bacon. The elements in his complex nature were so combined that he was seldom conscious of any clash between them. He could believe that he acted meanly from noble motives.

Bacon's life can only be understood if this complexity of character is kept constantly in view. We must remember, too, that his paradoxical combination of philanthropy and cynicism was stimulated by the intellectual and moral atmosphere of his age. That distrust of tradition which was natural to the new learning, a distrust which in the purely intellectual sphere was infinitely valuable, proving all things and holding fast that which was true, was a source of immediate danger in the moral sphere. After the break up of the mediæval Christian code of action came a time of chaos ; the intellect experimented and blundered towards the development of a new code, in which reason gave new authority to the best elements in the old. The justification of the means by the end was not doctrine of the Jesuits only. Statesmen caught up the same idea. Machiavelli's *Prince*, one of the most influential books of the Renascence, argued with very great power and subtlety for a statecraft based on exploitation of the weaknesses of men, turning them to account for government.

Two main characteristics emerge very early in Bacon's methods, both perfectly comprehensible in view of his character. He recognized that power was concentrated in the hands of a few, supremely in the hands of the sovereign ; and that the simplest practical means of reaching an end was often not the method ethically ideal. From the first premise it followed that the first step towards practical power was to secure the favour of one who held it. From the second it followed that the means of doing this were chosen for convenience. Truth and openness he recognized as the ideals of a statesman ; but ideals could not always be fulfilled. Bacon's first efforts towards promotion were directed partly to prove his capacity, partly to secure influential support, without which the highest merit might remain a beggar. He settled at Gray's Inn, and pursued his studies in law ; but his wish was to obtain some Crown office, not to practise at the Bar. He turned naturally for patronage to Lord Treasurer Burghley, his uncle by marriage. Exactly what employment he sought remains uncertain. In his first letter to Burghley he acknowledges " that the request is rare and unaccustomed," and declares " my hope of it resteth only upon your lordship's good affection towards me and grace with her Majesty." He concludes with a protestation of boundless gratitude and service in a style which grows familiar in his later letters : " I cannot account your lordship's service distinct from that which I owe to God and my Prince ; the performance whereof to best proof and purpose is the meeting-point and rendezvous of all my thoughts."

Bacon's next letter is full of gratitude to Burghley and to the Queen, who had promised " to vouchsafe to appropriate me into her service." But he was to find to his cost that both the Queen and her Minister were past-masters of that art of inexpensive promising which later he himself applauded : " Certainly, the politic and artificial nourishing and entertaining of hopes, and carrying men from hopes to hopes, is one of the best antidotes against the poison of discontentments." Bacon had to find such nourishment as he could in hope, for no office was given to him. He continued his studies, and was admitted " Utter Barrister " in 1582. Two years later came a first instalment of " satisfaction "; he was returned to Parliament for Melcombe Regis.

At this time, the chief care of Parliament was to secure the throne, and with it Protestantism, against the attacks of Papists. Fourteen years before, Pope Pius V. had issued a Bull of Excommunication, deposing the Queen ; and the intervening time had seen repeated plots against her rule and against her life. Elizabeth's death and the accession of Mary Stuart would have meant a return of Catholicism, or civil war ; and the quarrelling sects in Parliament made common cause against the Catholic, while patriotism stood to arms for the independence of England against the intrigues of Spain and of Rome. Parliament met in a fervour of Protestantism and patriotic enthusiasm. It sanctioned the " Bond of Association " by which subjects voluntarily bound themselves to defend the Queen, and put to death any person by whom or on whose behalf any attempt against her life should be made ; and new repressive measures against the Catholics were passed. At such critical times, it was the custom that any person of not too slight importance, who felt that he had valuable advice to offer, should address it to the sovereign or to a Minister of State. We have a letter to the Queen on the treatment of the Catholics, written probably about the end of 1584, which, though the evidence does not amount to proof, we may probably ascribe to Bacon. In this, his first recorded utterance on the attitude of the state towards sectarians, Bacon takes up the position from which he never wavered. He considers the situation purely from the political point of view, with statesmanlike impartiality. He could not appreciate the passionate strength of feeling with which the extremists on either side viewed the theological issue. His own religious feeling laid little stress on dogma ; indeed, it provided rather a supplement to his intellectual life than an essential element in it. The problem must thus have appeared to him simpler than it was. He advises a modification in the oath of allegiance, " to this sense : that whosoever would not bear arms against all foreign princes, and namely the Pope, that should in any way invade your Majesty's dominions, he should be a traitor." The issue is thus made political, not theological ; and recusants would be punished for treachery, not for Romanism. He further suggests unobtrusive measures to weaken the Catholic position : liberty to the Puritan preachers, whose departures from orthodox Anglicanism are outweighed by their powerful influence against Papistry ; supervision of education ; provision that no Catholic shall hold state office ; protection of Protestant tenants against Catholic landlords, and so on. More vigorous methods he deprecates as likely to drive Catholics to despair and desperate action. Above all, they must not be given the glory of martyrdom. " Compel them you would not, kill them you would not, so in reason trust them you would not."

Events soon justified, and in their issue removed, the urgency of the national mistrust of Catholics and fear of Spain. Mary Queen of Scots was executed in 1587, and the Armada was defeated in 1588. And with the removal, for the time at least, of the general danger to Protestantism, Protestants threw their released vigour again into their internal struggles. For thirty years the Puritans and the supporters of the middle way had been at strife. Archbishop Parker's demand for conformity had driven the first dissenters out of the Church. His successor, Grindal, on the other hand, had championed the cause of the moderate

Puritans against Elizabeth, and indeed was suspended for refusing to put down their meetings or " prophesyings." In 1583 Bacon's old tutor, Whitgift, became Archbishop, and renewed with great severity the attempt to enforce conformity. The defeat of the Armada, which removed the cause of temporary truce, was promptly followed by the publication of the Martin Marprelate tracts against the Archbishop ; and the theological issue lay, for the rest of Elizabeth's reign, between the rival sects of Protestants, not between Protestant and Catholic. Bacon had shown his attitude by some remarks in the *Letter of Advice* just discussed. " I am not given over, no, nor so much as addicted, to their preciseness ; therefore, till I think that you think otherwise [1] I am bold to think that the bishops in this dangerous time take a very evil and unadvised course in driving them from their cures " ; for, he proceeds, England's influence abroad must suffer through internal dissensions, and though " oversqueamish and nice," the Puritans are useful in " lessening and diminishing the Papistical number." The same attitude characterizes *An Advertisement touching the Controversies of the Church of England,* written in 1589.

Bacon was the son of a zealous Puritan, but the pupil of Whitgift. His intervention was as impartial as these circumstances would lead us to expect. His religious views had long troubled his mother. She warns Anthony against his advice and example in these matters ; and again, advising Anthony to pray with his servants twice daily, remarks " Your brother is too negligent therein." Bacon's intellectual temper was above all critical. It led him in theological affairs to a position somewhat aloof ; he surveyed the strife without real sympathy for either party, for he could see no essential importance in the questions at issue. The real problem for him was to find a settlement satisfactory, not to the theologians on either side, but to the statesman. He saw in the Puritan movement an important force, producing results

[1] Note the characteristic readiness to withdraw his opinion if it is distasteful

good and bad : making for righteousness and purity,
and potent against the political danger of Romanism ;
but making also for intellectual narrowness, for intoler-
ance, for impatience of authority, for a religion with the
fault he combated in philosophy—the fault of slavery
to words. He saw in the extreme Episcopalian movement another important force, making for law and
order, for a Church system harmonizing with the general
system of national government ; but at the same time
making for arbitrary action, for an arrogant self-satis-
faction which ignored just criticism, for worldliness and
laxity. His censures on both extremes were just; but
he failed to see that each side was fighting for principles
which it believed to be of the very first importance.
His solution was that of the finest common sense ; to
combine on essentials, to agree to differ on non-essentials, to remedy the serious evils in the established
system, and to leave liberty for intellectual differences
not dangerous to that system. But fortunately for the
soul, though unfortunately for the convenience of daily
life, there are matters in religion, even in dogma, beyond
the judgment of common sense. Bacon's cool and clear
intellect could not imagine a mind so dominated by
religious emotion that every detail of its belief, even
every circumstance of its worship, was important to it
beyond any worldly thing. Therefore his solution was
valueless to the intensely religious Puritan. Zealous for
order and authority as necessary conditions of sound
social organization, but intellectually an inveterate rebel
against merely traditional authority, he was incapable
of understanding a temper which held the law of the
Church sacred and unquestionable, and which viewed
dissent not merely as inconvenient to the State but
as attacking the foundations of religion. Therefore his
solution was valueless to the convinced Churchman.

It is natural to compare Bacon's *Advertisement touching the Controversies of the Church of England* with
Hooker's *Laws of Ecclesiastical Polity*, the first four
books of which appeared only five years later, in 1594.
Hooker is an apologist for the Anglican position, and

he does not recognize so clearly as does Bacon the moral worth of Puritanism, or the justice of its criticisms of the Church ; but he comes nearer than Bacon to understanding its religious basis. He sees that its essential claim is to individual responsibility to God, so that only the word of God can give its law. He sees in this claim the danger of the narrower tyranny of the Scriptures, and argues with all his magnificent resources of intellect and eloquence for the broader revelation of God through the laws of nature, the law of reason, the law of the Church, as well as the Bible. He arrives at a solution not dissimilar from Bacon's, though naturally more favourable to the Established Church ; but he bases his conclusions philosophically, recognizing the true meaning of the claim which he combats. Hooker writes of religion like a philosopher, though prejudiced by dogmatic prepossessions. Bacon writes of religion like a politician, though with the loftiest purposes and fine ethical feeling.

The wisdom and lucidity of the *Advertisement* must have suggested the employment of its author as apologist for the Government against criticism at home and abroad. For the relations of England with France, in particular, it was important that neither the Protestant nor the moderate Catholic party in France should be alienated by the attitude of the English Government towards English co-religionists. With this need in view, a letter was addressed to M. Critoy, "Secretary of France," over the signature of Walsingham ; in all probability its author was Bacon. He defends the moderation and consistency of the Government's treatment of Puritan and Catholic alike.

An apologist was again urgently needed in 1592, when a pamphlet called *Responsio ad Edictum Reginæ Angliæ* was published on the continent, attacking in unmeasured terms the Government's treatment of Roman Catholics. Bacon at once took the opportunity of a " device," or entertainment, given in honour of the Queen by Essex, probably on the anniversary of her coronation, to compose a " Discourse in Praise of

the Queen," in which her policy as well as her personal
qualities received eloquent eulogy. Before the year
ended, he gave a specific answer to the charges of the
Responsio in the weighty and closely reasoned *Observation on a Libel Published this present year* 1592.[1] Here
Bacon was driven to argue *ex parte ;* his business was
to offer a defence of Government action, and to deliver
a counter-attack on political Catholicism. He did his
work excellently, but the paper necessarily lacks the
fine balance and impartiality which make his general
discussions of the theological situation so attractive
and so valuable.

CHAPTER II

BACON AND ESSEX : THE DAYS OF STRUGGLE

DURING the years covered by these difficulties of the
Government in the religious settlement, Bacon had continued legal work, and in 1586 had become a " bencher "
of Gray's Inn, with the right to plead in the Courts at
Westminster. Still promotion passed him by. Burghley
continued to flatter his hopes, but for some unknown
reason—it may have been merely personal antipathy—
never exerted himself on his behalf. Bacon grew weary
of waiting. One of his motives in seeking Government
employment was to gain influence for the promotion of
a great project which he had long been meditating—
nothing less than the fundamental reform of Knowledge.
Delay in preferment meant not only disappointment of
natural ambition, but waste of time in pursuing his
greater ulterior purpose. " I wax now somewhat
ancient," he writes to Burghley, presumably in 1592,
" one and thirty years is a great deal of sand in the
hour-glass. . . . I confess that I have as vast contemplative ends, as I have moderate civil ends : for I
have taken all knowledge to be my province ; and if
I could purge it of two sorts of rovers, whereof the one

[1] Written in January or February, therefore 1593 in modern
reckoning.

with frivolous disputations, computations, and verbosities, the other with blind experiments and auricular traditions and impostures, hath committed so many spoils, I hope I should bring in industrious observations, grounded conclusions, and profitable inventions and discoveries; the best state of that province. . . . And I do easily see that place of any reasonable countenance doth bring commandment of more wits than a man's own; which is the thing I greatly affect. . . . And if your Lordship will not carry me on . . . I will sell the inheritance that I have, and purchase some lease of quick revenue . . . and so give over all care of service, and become some sorry book-maker, or a true pioneer in that mine of truth."

Just before this letter was written, in the mood which it depicts, Bacon had made the acquaintance of the Earl of Essex. Essex was the rising star at the Court. He had gained Elizabeth's favour with astonishing rapidity, and though he was only twenty-five, his brilliant and attractive personality made him a serious rival to the stolidly worthy Burghley. Burghley may well have distrusted Bacon for his very wealth of ideas, and for his bookish interests. Essex, himself a student of adventurous mind, was singularly well qualified to appreciate these qualities. To Bacon, weary of begging favours from a man for whose intellect he must have felt some contempt, Essex must have appeared the ideal patron, and further acquaintance for a time confirmed his hopes. Essex was as generous practically as intellectually; as zealous to serve his friends as he was quick to understand their ideas. In him united all the graces and many of the powers of the ideal Elizabethan; he lacked only the strength and balance of character to bear success unspoiled. His tragedy is the converse of Bacon's; Bacon's character was confirmed in its worst parts and crippled in some noble possibilities by adverse circumstances; success betrayed Essex into a sensitive self-assertiveness and an impatience of authority which at last ruined him.

This new and powerful patronage might well have

gained prompt promotion for Bacon, had not a situation
arisen in which political honesty compelled him to
stand against the Queen and the Government. When
Parliament met in February 1593, the Government
urgently needed money to combat a Spanish plot in
Scotland. The Committee of the Commons recognized
the need, and voted two subsidies instead of the usual
one ; but Burghley regarded this as insufficient, and
not only demanded three subsidies, but also declared
that the amount should be determined in conference
with the Lords. This proposal struck at the very root
of the power of the Lower House—its absolute control
of supply ; and the same regard for order in the State
which had inspired Bacon's writings on the Church
settlement now drove him to lead the opposition to this
demand. The Government found it advisable to drop
the plan of a Conference, but still urged that the three
subsidies should be paid in four years instead of six
years. Bacon again objected, on the ground that
taxation thus concentrated into the briefer time would
impose too heavy a burden on the country, and further
would create a dangerous precedent unless distinctly
noted as extraordinary. The Commons, however, were
satisfied with their victory on the point of principle,
and Bacon stood alone in opposition. Burghley demanded an explanation. Instead of apologizing, Bacon
justified his attitude in terms at once modest and
dignified : " The manner of my speech did most evi-
dently show that I spake simply and only to satisfy
my conscience, and not with any advantage or policy
to sway the cause ; and my terms carried all signi-
fication of duty and zeal towards her Majesty and her
service."

This incident, entirely creditable to Bacon's character, raised a new obstacle to his promotion. No
honesty of motive could justify opposition to Elizabeth or her ministers. In a great minister it had sometimes to be tolerated, but in a candidate for office it
was presumption deserving sharp punishment. For
some time Bacon found it advisable to avoid the Court,

trusting that the Queen might forgive him when she had in part forgotten the offence. Just at this inopportune moment the Mastership of the Rolls fell vacant, and brought into prospect a change in the office of Attorney-General. Bacon gained the intercession of his cousin, Sir Thomas Cecil, with Burghley, and Essex sued urgently and persistently on his behalf. In another letter to Burghley, though still he will not apologize, Bacon expresses regret for the impression his action has made on the Queen. One bitter phrase shows that he has learned the lesson of the incident : in future, if he cannot give unquestioning support to the royal policy, he will at least abstain from unwelcome comment. " If the not seconding of some particular person's opinion shall be presumption, and to differ upon the manner shall be to impeach the end, it shall teach my devotion not to exceed wishes, and those in silence."

These efforts gradually dispersed the Queen's active disfavour, but they could not gain Bacon the Attorney-Generalship. His rival for the office was Edward Coke, a great and unscrupulous lawyer, who as Speaker of the House of Commons had used all his influence for Government in the very debate where Bacon showed such obnoxious independence. It was the first incident in a lifelong hostility between the two men, and Coke scored the first point. The Solicitor-Generalship now fell vacant. For this too Bacon applied, and again, after more than a year's delay, it was given elsewhere. The disappointment left Bacon in a position almost desperate. He was heavily in debt, for his income was quite inadequate to the position which he had to keep up at Court. His brother Anthony had disposed of an estate to help him, but Anthony's own financial position was now embarrassed. Essex came to the rescue with characteristic magnificence of generosity, and gave Bacon land worth £1800.[1] " You fare ill because you have chosen me for your mean and dependence ; you have spent your time and thoughts in my matter. I die if I do not somewhat towards your fortune ; you

[1] Multiply by seven to give modern equivalent value.

shall not deny to accept a piece of land which I will bestow upon you." Bacon, after some demur, accepted the gift, and gratefully named himself Essex's "homager." " But do you know the manner of doing homage in law ? " he added, qualifying the term—" Always it is with a saving of his faith to his king and his other lords ; and therefore, my lord, I can be no more yours than I was, and it must be with the ancient savings."

But while obligations bound Bacon more and more closely to Essex, his confidence that he had found an ideal patron must have already become troubled. The phrases just quoted [1] suggest the recognition that Essex's desires might not always harmonize with the good of the State. Already Essex had, on several occasions, shown himself too headstrong for a statesman. This, coupled with his practical disappointments, made Bacon feel hopeless of the career he had planned, and he wrote to Essex : " I am purposed not to follow the practice of the law . . . because it drinketh too much time, which I have dedicated to better purposes. . . . For your Lordship, I do think myself more beholding to you than to any man. And I say I reckon myself as a *common* (not popular, but *common*) ; and as much as is lawful to be enclosed of a common, so much your Lordship shall be sure to have." [2]

---

[1] Their value is diminished by the fact that they are drawn from Bacon's own account, published nine years later to justify his abandonment of Essex.

[2] The last sentence is interesting. It has generally been interpreted in the sense which Bacon later put upon it for his own justification, as implying " a significant reserve of his devotion " to Essex. But may it not well refer to the " better purposes " to which Bacon proposed to dedicate his time ? " I reckon myself a common "—the property of the community ; does not this mean that he holds his talents in trust for the general good, and feels that he dare not devote to any individual more than "is lawful" of the powers which it is his duty to employ for the benefit of mankind ? The phrase may apply to political and personal service, without any special foreboding of a clash between the service of Essex and that of the State. The clash is rather between the service of temporary ends and that of the permanent general

Still, even when further disappointments followed, when he was passed over for the Mastership of the Rolls, and again outstripped by Coke, this time as suitor to the rich young widow of Sir Christopher Hatton, Bacon did not follow this impulse to give up his original plans and devote himself solely to philosophical work. He clung to the hope of office, growing steadily more cynical in his view of the means by which success must be gained. Essex's brilliant success in the capture of Cadiz, in 1596, seemed to him ominous rather than auspicious; for he feared that it would make Essex new enemies at Court, and still more that the Queen would distrust his growing power and popularity with the army and with the people. Bacon accordingly wrote an elaborate letter of advice to Essex. " Win the Queen; if this be not the beginning, of any other course I see no end "; and he sets forth a number of ways in which Essex should shape his behaviour and his actions. The advice holds much common sense, but savours unpleasantly of conscious trickiness and courtier's cunning. And, though it recognizes the dangerous elements in Essex's character and position, it fails to suggest a course of action possible to him. His virtues and his faults alike unfitted him for careful court intrigue; it was largely by his daring independence that he had gained the Queen's favour. The character of his relations with the Queen made his position particularly difficult. He had to display the privileged familiarity of the personal favourite, or the instant submission of the courtier, according to Elizabeth's mood. When plans were being made for " The Island Voyage," to strike a further blow against Spain, in 1597, his jealousy of Lord Howard and of Sir Walter Raleigh caused new friction with the Queen, who " had resolved to break him of his will and pull down his great heart." The expedition was a failure,

progress of mankind. *Cf.* the opening sentence of *De Interpretatione Naturæ Proœmium.* On the closing phrase I may echo a MS. comment of the late Professor Charles Rowley : " How much of a common is it lawful to enclose ? "

and he returned, discontented and in disfavour, to play
into his enemies' hands.

At this time affairs in Ireland were in a very disquieting
state.   Hugh O'Neil, Earl of Tyrone, an old rebel against
the harsh English yoke, a general who knew how to use
all the great advantages of his country in guerilla warfare, and a shrewd and unscrupulous politician, kept
up a series of rebellions which threatened at last to
spread through the whole country.   The negotiations
with him offered an opportunity for making a reputation
in the Council, and in March 1598, Bacon advised Essex
to " devote special attention to the question."   The
negotiations fell through ; and after a violent quarrel
with the Queen over the appointment of a commander-
in-chief for the new campaign, Essex himself was
ordered to the post.   A far greater soldier than he,
Sir John Norreys, had already failed to suppress the
rebellion ; and only an optimist with an exaggerated
notion of his own powers could have hoped for glory
from the undertaking.   Bacon had repeatedly urged
Essex to avoid military employment and to seek civil
office.   He claimed later that he advised Essex to avoid
the command in Ireland.   The only extant letter on
the subject, however, encourages Essex to go ; setting
forth the very great difficulties and dangers of the undertaking, but noting the glory, and still more the patriotic
service, of success.   It is important to determine
Bacon's attitude, for, while his later conduct was at best
ungenerous, it was dastardly if he had urged Essex to
take the risk.   Professor Gardiner thinks it possible that
Bacon wrote an earlier letter, urging Essex to refuse,
and that this has been lost.   On the other hand, Sir
Sidney Lee suggests that Bacon advised Essex to go,
with heartless indifference to the results of failure :
" His patron's case, as it presented itself to Bacon's
tortuous mind, was one of kill or cure . . . Bacon,
from his point of view, thought it desirable that Essex
should have the opportunity of achieving some definite
triumph in life which would render his future influence
supreme.   Or, if he were incapable of conspicuous

success in life, then the more patent his inefficiency became, and the quicker he was set on one side the better for his protégé's future."[1] The second, harsher view may be dismissed; for military success would not have secured Essex's position with the Queen, as Bacon had clearly recognized in his letter to the earl after the capture of Cadiz; and on the other hand, mere military failure might have left Essex's position little worse if he had behaved discreetly to the Queen. Without supposing the loss of an earlier letter, we may believe that Bacon's attitude remained unchanged; he feared the results of Essex's military employment, but recognized the hopelessness of dissuading him, and contented himself with mingling as much warning as possible with his forecast. He wrote the letter only on invitation: "Your late note of my silence on your occasion hath made me set down these few wandering lines." His faith in Essex was growing feebler, his confidence in the weight of his own advice had suffered since Essex had not followed earlier advice; and he let things go, with mingled hope and grave foreboding.

Essex completely failed to subdue the rebels; he never even engaged them seriously, and after wasting his forces in five months' blundering, desultory warfare, he proposed peace, on terms very favourable to Tyrone, in September. Despatches from the Queen had forbidden him to return without orders, but in the face of them he left Ireland and sought the Queen at Norwich. It must be remembered that he feared the intrigues of his enemies in his absence; he at first intended "to carry with him so much of the army as he could conveniently transport," and actually was accompanied as far as London by "the main part of his household and a great part of captains and gentlemen." That he cherished any project hostile to the Queen herself is altogether improbable; but he lost his head, and trusted by violent means to defeat his

---

[1] *Great Englishmen of the 16th Century*, p. 272. Here, and again on p. 43, I have expressly noted my disagreement with Sir Sidney Lee, because his opinion is too weighty to be ignored.

enemies, who, headed by Cecil, outplayed him at every
point in the game of wits. The Queen was thoroughly
displeased, and with justice ; but she was not disin-
clined to receive him again into favour when she had
thoroughly humiliated him. Essex could not endure
the uncertainty of his position and the constant pricks
to his pride. By January 1601, he and his friends
had formed a plot to surprise the Court, seize the Queen's
person, and compel her to dismiss from the Council Cecil,
Raleigh, and other enemies, and to grant other demands.
Discovery precipitated their action ; on February 8th,
accompanied by some two hundred gentlemen, on foot,
armed only with swords, he marched to Paul's Cross,
and tried to raise the people to his support. He failed.
Instead of attempting to escape he returned to Essex
House, perhaps to burn incriminating papers. About
ten o'clock the same night he was a prisoner.

Up to this time Bacon's conduct had been consistently friendly to Essex, though his line of action was
complicated by the difficulty of serving him without
offending the Queen. Bacon's position was extraordinarily delicate. In September 1598, he had been
arrested for debt ; so that clearly he had reached the
limits of his resources, and needed to clutch desperately
at any chance of mending his fortunes. And now at
last he seemed to be gaining Court favour ; he had
been appointed a Queen's Counsel, and had been given
intermittent work for Government. By bitter experience he had learned the cost of opposition to the
Queen. He had therefore to preserve the appearance
of unreserved zeal for the Queen, while serving Essex
as far as possible within these limits. He may well
have felt, too, that he would serve Essex ill by rashly
sacrificing his newly-gained influence. It was Bacon's
nature to prefer an intricate, " managing " course of
action to one perfectly straightforward. Finally, as
a statesman, he must have felt that such action as
Essex's disobedient and blustering return from Ireland
needed sharp correction, however much he desired to
shield his patron. The earl's party was strong enough

to threaten serious danger; and popular sympathy with him had been aroused on his return by his confinement, without trial, in York House. When the judicial inquiry was held, therefore, Bacon took an active part for the Government, but attempted to mitigate the charge against Essex. The very day after, he found opportunity to intercede for him with the Queen. He stated his position frankly in a letter to Essex: " I humbly pray you to believe that I aspire to the conscience and commendation first of *bonus civis*, which with us is a good and true servant to the Queen, and next of *bonus vir*, that is an honest man. I desire your Lordship to think that although I confess I love some things much better than I love your Lordship, as the Queen's service, her quiet and contentment, her honour, her favour, the good of my country, and the like, yet I love few persons better than yourself, both for gratitude's sake, and for your own virtues, which cannot hurt but by accident or abuse. Of which my good affection I was ever and am ready to yield testimony by any good offices, but with such reservations as yourself cannot but allow."

Essex answered in dignified and not unfriendly terms, and during the next three months freely used Bacon's services towards re-establishing his position with the Queen. Labouring thus to please both parties, Bacon pleased neither. Essex's friends were ignorant of his honest efforts to assuage the Queen's anger, and popular rumour accused him of aggravating the charge. He was even threatened with violence; he writes, with something of Roman temper, " I thank God I have the privy coat of a good conscience, and have a good while since put off any fearful care of life and the accidents of life." At the same time, the Queen thought him half-hearted in her service, and over-persistent in his suggestions in favour of Essex. In his conduct up to the rebellion, then, Bacon appears, not indeed as a hero ready to sacrifice everything for his friend, but certainly as loyal to him, under very trying circumstances, within the bounds of his duty to the State.

The mad attempt at armed rebellion entirely changed Bacon's attitude. Until then Bacon had probably regarded Essex as headstrong, lacking in political sagacity, needing careful restraint and guidance, but still a worse enemy to himself than to any other man ; and though his early hopes must have vanished completely, he respected the ties of gratitude which bound him to his benefactor.

By his rebellion Essex became a criminal against the State. Inquiry into his motives and intentions relieves him from the worst construction that might be put upon his action. In all probability he intended merely to purge the Government of the men whom he regarded as evil advisers to the Queen as well as personal enemies of his own. But no explanation can alter the fact that he attempted, by armed violence, to seize the person of his Queen, and to force her, against her own will and judgment, to dismiss her chosen ministers ; and this not in obedience to the will of a great section of the people, not to avoid any imminent peril to the State, but merely on his private judgment, influenced by his personal ambitions and enmities. Admiration of Essex's chivalrous nature, sympathy for the great noble flattered and flouted by the most difficult of royal mistresses, indignant pity for the simpler character befooled by cleverer players at the game of court intrigue, awe at the sudden, tragic end of such brilliant promise, all these we may feel ; and yet we must recognize that Essex was a traitor to the State, and struck at the very foundations of government.

In most political matters Bacon judged with cool reason and acted with a view to convenience ; but he had one political passion—for order, for the law and system which are necessary conditions of existence for an organized State. This passion had been fostered by his upbringing among statesmen, and had directed his own ambition to seek the greatest and worthiest sphere of practical power in service of the State. It had been fostered by his early experience in France, where he had seen the chaos produced by the method of arbitrary violence which Essex had attempted to employ. It had appeared in his letters of advice on the treatment of Puritan and Catholic, and in his resistance to the Queen's encroachments on the prerogative of the Commons. And while in the last case he recognized the authority of Parliament, and urged the most careful preservation of its rights, he preserved his final allegiance solely to the sovereign, whose authority he traced to divine sanction. The sovereign was for him the embodiment of the principle of government ; and no personal disappointment could touch his devoted loyalty, not to her person, but to her office. Essex had attempted the worst crime that Bacon could conceive, and he was bound to condemn the crime absolutely, and to wish that the criminal's power of repeating it should be broken.

But meaner motives mingled with patriotism, and drove Bacon to show in the prosecution of Essex an activity which disowned gratitude and loyal friendship, and even common decency. He was appointed to assist Coke, the Attorney-General, in conducting the prosecution. Twice Coke blundered in his attack, and each time Bacon intervened, blocking the side issues which were leading discussion to matters less dangerous to Essex, and levelling deadly comment against the weaknesses of the defence. Patriotism did not demand that he should persecute his friend to the death. Even without Bacon's intervention there was little chance that the sentence of the Court would leave Essex dangerous. Indeed, Bacon might well have used his magnificent oratory on his behalf, not to excuse his crime, but to plead for mitigation of the penalty, without failing in any duty to Queen or State. Instead, he flung himself into the prosecution with a power which compels admiration in the midst of disgust. Fear, passionate disappointment, the feeling that he had been deceived, ambition, all snatched the excuse of his shocked patriotism, like plundering cut-throats disgracing a noble cause. He must have feared that

he might be suspected of complicity in the plot, for he
had been pleading for Essex with the Queen throughout the long uncertain months before the plot, and his
brother Anthony, who was known to be on confidential
terms with Essex, had carried treasonable letters to
the King of Scotland. His early devotion was based
on the hope that Essex would further his projects, and
instead the ideal patron had appeared as the enemy
of his fundamental political principle. He had just
cause to feel deceived. At the very time when he was
drafting letters to the Queen for Essex, and helping
him, at the risk of the Queen's anger, by directing his
efforts to regain favour, Essex had been engaged in
treasonable intrigue with the Scots king. Against all
these feelings there weighed in favour of Essex only a
cool and reasonable recognition of favours received,
which Bacon believed he had already more than recom-
pensed. "I have been much bound unto him," he
wrote to Lord Henry Howard, before the plot, "And
on the other side, I have spent more time and more
thoughts about his well-doing than ever I did about
mine own." Warm personal feeling—gratitude or friendship beyond the just balance of debit and credit—was
alien to his nature. All the force of circumstance
worked with his feelings against Essex. It would have
been difficult for him to refuse at least nominal concern
in the prosecution ; for though he was merely one of
the Queen's Counsel, he had been employed by the
Government particularly in connection with political
plots, and had already acted formally against Essex in
the proceedings connected with the Irish campaign.
Finally, it is hard not to suspect one particularly ungenerous motive. His rival Coke, whom he hated as
thoroughly as so poor a lover could hate, was officially
in charge of the prosecution ; and rivalry and ambition
alike must have prompted Bacon to eclipse his leader.
His second intervention seems especially designed to
criticize Coke's blundering conduct of the case. "I
have never yet seen in any case such favour shown
to any prisoner ; so many digressions, such delivering

of evidence by fractions, and so silly a defence of such great and notorious treasons." Then comes the display of his own powers, in contrast with those of Coke ; a brief summary of Essex's defence, answered point by point with deadly effect :

" Put the case that the Earl of Essex's intents were, as he would have it believed, to go only as a suppliant to her Majesty. Should their petitions be presented by armed petitioners ? This must needs bring loss of liberty to the prince. Neither is it any point of law, as my Lord Southampton would have it believed, that condemns them of treason. To take secret counsel, to execute it, to run together in numbers armed with weapons—what can be the excuse ? Warned by the Lord Keeper, by a herald, and yet persist ! Will any simple man take this to be less than treason ? "

Essex was condemned, and under the influence of Ashton, a Puritan preacher, made a strange and pathetic confession of his guilt. He was executed on February 25, 1601. Out of the fines and forfeitures to the Crown by Essex's fellow-rebels, Bacon received £1200 ; not as much as he hoped, he writes to a creditor. Some six years earlier Essex had given him an estate worth £1800.

Later, when the death of Elizabeth had changed political conditions, he published an " Apology," an explanation and defence of his actions, setting forth very forcibly all that can be said in his favour. But even here we find no evidence that Bacon's action cost him struggle and pain, or that it caused him remorse. It is not difficult to understand Bacon's action, and justice compels us to recognize one great and worthy motive among the forces which drove him to it. But in this case to understand is not to forgive. Essex was a traitor to the laws which make possible a civilized and organized state, and by those laws he deserved death. Bacon was a traitor to higher laws than these—the laws of honour, of pity, of love ; and by those sacred laws he stands condemned.

CHAPTER III

BACON AND JAMES I. : THE DAYS OF PROSPERITY

THE remaining years of Elizabeth's reign were comparatively unimportant in Bacon's life. In May 1601, died his brother Anthony—the only person for whom he ever showed sincere affection ; and Bacon inherited from him enough to meet his most urgent financial needs. In statesmanship he displayed his usual wisdom and foresight. He introduced into Parliament a bill to amend the system of weights and measures. He urged the repeal of superfluous laws. On the vexed question of monopolies, he distinguished acutely between the patents granted for useful discoveries, and those merely conferring an unearned right of monopoly. In Irish affairs, he advised, among more familiar and somewhat Machiavellian means of pacification, a policy of support to education and of complete toleration in religion. He introduced a bill amending the method of settling disputes in assurances among merchants. Nothing else need be recorded until Elizabeth's death and the accession of James I. in 1603.

Under Elizabeth two habits of Bacon's political thought had grown into second nature. By temperament he was attracted by a devious "managing" policy, and in Elizabeth he watched a past mistress of the art treating most difficult problems of internal and external policy with wonderful success. He venerated the office of sovereign as symbol and source of firm government and order. The strength which underlay Elizabeth's shiftiness had justified and reinforced his veneration ; while the difficulty of gaining her favour, and the relentless punishment which followed opposition to her will, had whipped the place-seeker in Bacon into a sense of the convenience of serving the monarch at any cost. He was now forty-three, and still stood only on a lower rung of the ladder to success. His appetite for power had been only whetted by the scraps of office which fell to him. His honesty was corroded by disappointment, and flawed by years of time-serving; and his just consciousness of his own great gifts, confirmed by proof, was irritated by continued failure to gain adequate employment. With his personal ambition burned, with a brighter flame, his passionate desire to serve his country and his kind, to carry into effect his dreams of statesmanship and of the conquest of nature by knowledge. A prophet may be as unscrupulous as an adventurer.

The accession of James thus found Bacon with the noblest elements in his nature allied with the ignoble in desperate desire for power, seeking it at the fountain-head, the Crown. It is not easy to decide how far his flattery of the King was merely diplomatic—it certainly exceeded the limits of decent diplomacy—and how far it was due to his eagerness to believe what he wished to be true. His hopes may have transfigured James's pedantry into sympathy towards learning, his arrogant assumption into strength, his love of argument into accessibility to advice. More probably he had decided to win the King's favour by any means available. He gave good advice, but if it proved unwelcome he modified it. The strongest intellect of the day grovelled in flattery before a bladder in which a few peas of prejudice rattled noisily. The man who had dared to oppose Elizabeth became obsequious to her feeble and foolish successor.

In his renewed struggle for place, Bacon even tried to obtain support from some of Essex's friends; perhaps not so much from audacity as because he felt satisfied with his own excuses for his actions, and believed that others would recognize their justice. At first his hopes were once more disappointed. Burghley's son and successor in office, Robert Cecil, seems to have been as unwilling as his father to employ Bacon; and his old rival Coke, by this time recognized as the greatest lawyer of his day, also stood between him and office. The King scattered honours freely, but none fell to

Bacon. After being arrested a second time for debt, he wrote to Cecil, who had lent him money to obtain release, in terms recalling those of earlier, despondent letters :

"For my purpose or course, I desire to meddle as little as I can in the King's causes, his Majesty now abounding in counsel ; and to follow my private thrift and practice, and to marry with some convenient advancement. For as for any ambition, I do assure your Honour, mine is quenched. . . . My ambition now I shall only put upon my pen, whereby I shall be able to maintain memory and merit of the times succeeding."

Bacon never lost sight of his vision of man's conquest of nature, and his desire to prepare the way for it never wavered. But the search for office, at first only as a necessary stage to the higher end, grew so eager that it often obscured that end ; and since Bacon failed to achieve success early enough to set free his mature years for his true life work, we welcome the times when he turned wearily from chasing the butterfly of promotion to tend the swarming hive of his philosophical ideas.

An introductory address to his work *On the Interpretation of Nature* was probably written now. Through alterations in his general scheme, Bacon never published it ; but we shall refer to it later at some length for its fine statement of his ideals and motives, alike as philosopher and statesman. At this time, too, he probably began his great work on *The Advancement of Learning.*

In the letter to Cecil from which we have just quoted, Bacon begs for "this divulged and almost prostituted honour of knighthood." His request was granted, but not the prayer "that the manner might be such as might grace me, since the matter will not ; I mean, that I might not be merely gregarious in a troop." He was knighted with three hundred others, without distinction, two days before the Coronation. But with the assembling of James's first Parliament came opportunities for Bacon to serve and gratify King and Commons alike. Repeatedly his tact saved friction between them ; and his work on the problems raised by the proposed political union of England and Scotland was both statesmanlike in its principles, and diplomatic in its attitude towards over-hasty King and over-cautious English subjects. In the earlier disputes between King and Commons, arising from fundamental differences between their respective conceptions of royal rights, disputes which were to grow still angrier, Bacon acted as mediator ; and no man could have been better fitted for the delicate task. He venerated the law as the instrument of social order ; he venerated the sovereign as the divinely appointed agent of authority. He believed that the King's rights were independent of law, but that righteousness, wisdom, and convenience all directed him to govern according to law.

While thus strengthening his position in State affairs, he found time, in the intervals of civil employment, to complete the two books of *The Advancement of Learning*, dedicated to the King, published in 1605. James, with his narrow, superficial vision, and his schoolman's wordy and pedantic philosophy, could not appreciate the wide sweep of Bacon's thought nor its demand for a firm basis in facts. Nor did any success attend a letter written earlier in the same year to Lord Chancellor Ellesmere, urging the encouragement of work on English history.

Though the value of his Parliamentary services was known, recognition by office still delayed. In 1604 he had been raised from the ranks of unsalaried Learned Counsel to be a King's Counsel by patent, with a salary of £60 a year ; but he was not employed by Government in the first trial of Raleigh, nor in connection with the Gunpowder Plot. In 1606 he married Alice Barnham, the " alderman's daughter, an handsome maiden, to my liking," of whom he had written to Cecil three years earlier. Her fortune was, however, inadequate to keep up the magnificent style of living which his Renascence temper demanded—a style illustrated by his wedding preparations. " Sir Francis Bacon," wrote a contemporary, " was married yesterday to his young wench, in Maribone Chapel. He was clad from top to toe

in purple, and hath made himself and his wife such store
of raiments of cloth of silver and gold that it draws deep
nto her portion." His need of promotion was greater
than ever, " to satisfy his wife's friends " as well as to fulfil
his own ambitions. In 1606 the Attorney-Generalship
fell vacant, and in the consequent shuffling of offices
Bacon hoped to be made Solicitor-General. He appealed to the King, recounting his services and recalling
his obedience. Once again disappointment awaited him.
The Solicitor-Generalship did not immediately become
vacant, and it was not until June 1607, that he received the appointment. It was worth about £1000 a
year. With this the tide of fortune at last turned.
In the following year there fell to him the Registrar-
ship of the Star Chamber, the reversion of which he
had been given by Burghley nineteen years before.
This was worth some £1600, and his total income now
amounted, according to his own estimate, to £4975 a
year.[1] Unluckily, his style of living always moved a
little in advance of his fortune ; he still needed more
money. And the success so long delayed had little
savour ; perhaps he vaguely felt its vanity, perhaps it
was only that he had time to feel tired. "I have found
now twice, upon amendment of my fortune, disposition
to melancholy and distaste. . . . Upon my Solicitor's
place I grew indisposed and inclined to superstition.
Now . . . I find a relapse into my old symptoms, as I was
wont to have it many years ago."

Immediately after his appointment as Registrar to
the Star Chamber he used the leisure of a week in the
Long Vacation to jot down reflections and notes on the
matters occupying his mind, personal, political, and
philosophical. These memoranda (*Commentarius Sol-
utus*) were intended solely for his private convenience,
and offer a record as naked and unselfconscious as the
diary of Pepys. The personal notes are naturally the
most interesting ; much of the matter of those dealing
with philosophical problems or with affairs of State found
fuller and more careful expression in published work.

[1] About £35,000 in modern money

THE DAYS OF PROSPERITY 39

Bacon's work as Solicitor-General does not call for detailed comment. He discharged his legal duties with very great ability, displaying wide and exact knowledge of the law, and interpreting it liberally. Indeed, his readiness to sacrifice the letter to the spirit brought him into frequent conflict with Coke, who was still more learned in law, and who carried precision into pedantry. Bacon prepared reports on the Penal Laws, striking in the lucidity of their presentment of facts and wise in their recommendations for reform. He set his face resolutely against duelling; later, as Attorney-General, he continued this attack on an evil custom, and obtained a decree from the Star Chamber making a challenge to a duel, even if not accepted, a punishable offence. He again urged his views on Irish affairs, developing his earlier advice. In the stormy discussions of the "Great Contract," he played a useful though thankless part. By this scheme of Salisbury's, the King was to surrender certain traditional privileges, from which he derived income, including those of "wardship" and "purveyance," and to abandon "impositions"—arbitrary taxes, unsanctioned by the Commons, on imports. In return the Commons were to grant the King a sum of at least £500,000 towards the royal debt, which his extravagance had greatly increased, and to promise a further annual payment. James acted from the first like a huckster, in the end like a sharper, attempting to capture the grant, but to delay his concessions until further payment had been extorted. Bacon had to appear as the friend of both sides, championing the Commons as their spokesman, and aiding the King's cause as his servant. He worked zealously and skilfully to give the best possible form to a scheme which he did not like, and to find ground for a settlement by mutual accommodation. Though he affirmed the privileges of the King, he urged the wisdom of compromise. But the most skilful handling could not save the scheme; it was foredoomed to failure by James's arrogance and dishonesty.

In all the pressure of legal and political work Bacon

never lost sight of his plans for the new foundation of knowledge. About 1607 he wrote the dissertation on things thought and seen, *Cogitata et Visa*, setting forth his reflections on the evidence of his experience; and in 1609 his antipathy to tradition found outlet in a brilliant though unbalanced attack on the classic philosophies, *Redargutio Philosophiarum*. A letter to his friend Andrewes, with the MS. of the first-named work, explains Bacon's motive in writing these fragments—to crystallize his thoughts in essays later to be superseded by a complete and ordered treatise, the *Great Instauration*: " I send you some of this vacation's fruits; and thus much more of my mind and purpose. I hasten not to publish; perishing I would prevent. And I am forced to respect as well my times as the matter. For with me it is thus, and I think with all men in my case : if I bind myself to an argument, it loadeth my mind ; but if I rid my mind of the present cogitation, it is rather a recreation. This hath put me into these miscellanies ; which I propose to suppress, if God give me leave to write a just and perfect volume of philosophy, which I go on with, though slowly."

While Bacon was thus labouring with faithful love in his self-appointed service of knowledge and truth, events were preparing which plunged him more deeply and more discreditably into affairs. In May 1612, Salisbury died. " From this date," writes Dean Church, " James passed from government by a minister, who, whatever may have been his faults, was laborious, public-spirited, and a statesman, into his own keeping and into the hands of favourites, who cared only for themselves. With Cecil [Lord Salisbury] ceased the traditions of the days of Elizabeth and Burghley, in many ways evil and cruel traditions, but not ignoble and sordid ones ; and James was left without the stay, and also without the check, which Cecil's power had been to him." Bacon at once offered the King his services as political adviser, urging very justly his special qualifications to mediate between Crown and Commons : " Though no man can say but I was a perfect and peremptory royalist, yet every man makes me believe that I was never one hour out of credit with the lower house." Mindful, doubtless, of Bacon's usefulness in the debates on the Great Contract, James accepted the offer. The series of papers which Bacon accordingly prepared is admirably characterized by Professor S. R. Gardiner. " There is in them too much respect for mere management, and too strong an inclination to regard the opposition to the King as in the main personal. Yet, on the whole, the ground they take is unassailable. There is to be no more bargaining between king and subjects. The King is to show his determination to lead in the right direction, and to be content to wait until his subjects are prepared to follow. He is not to press for supply, but to wait until the Commons are sufficiently impressed with his devotion to the nation to offer him all that he needs. . . . To carry out this programme would have been to avert the evils of the next half-century. No one to whose mind the history of that half-century is present can agree with those numerous writers who speak of Bacon's political work as inferior to his scientific. He was the one man capable of preventing a catastrophe by antici-pating the demands of the age. . . . Unhappily, he could not procure acceptance for his political ideas."

As the gulf gradually widened between James and Parliament, it became increasingly difficult to reconcile obedience to the King with true service of the State. By his declaration of belief in Divine Right, Bacon had already pledged himself to the King's service. He strengthened his bonds by pressing for new office. With the death of Salisbury, who had always stood in his way, Bacon's hopes rose higher. His enmity to Salis-bury found expression in letters to the King criticizing and blaming Salisbury's policy, accusing him of thwarting the King's purposes, and offering his own obsequious service in whatever post the King might confer on him : " I will be ready as a chessman to be wherever your Majesty's royal hand shall set me." Bacon had reason enough to dislike Salisbury ; but sympathy is alienated by the contrast between his repeated professions of unbounded devotion to Salisbury during his life, and this bitter censure as soon as he could no longer reward or punish. Dean Church throws out the suggestion that James may have "disclosed something of his dead servant which showed his unsuspected hostility to Bacon." More probably Bacon's enmity was long cherished ; but with Salisbury in power Bacon had nothing to gain by an open quarrel, and might hope for reward if his flattering protestations could gain belief. It is the method of Machiavelli again ; and again we must infer a weakness in Bacon's moral constitution.

Once more Bacon had to endure disappointment before he gained promotion ; but, though James valued Bacon's wise advice on high principles of government little more than his plans for the advancement of learning, he could appreciate his skilful and not over-scrupulous service in Parliament. The Attorney-Generalship fell vacant, and Bacon received the appointment on October 27, 1613. He had hoped for this very appointment, under Essex's patronage, twenty years before. For twenty years he had been driven and tossed between hope and disappointment. For twenty years he had spent himself in true and worthy service, and had intrigued deviously for the reward which merit alone did not gain. Intending to make his lower ambitions serve his highest ideals, in twenty years he had learnt to subordinate the higher to the lower, to make a necessity of what should have been merely a convenience. Shaping his conduct consistently towards certain ends, he had grown increasingly careless of the means ; guiding his life by the standard of reason, he had grown callous to the better half of human nature.

Measured by his early hopes the success he had gained at fifty-two was failure. He had dreamed of serving his country greatly as adviser of a great ruler ; instead, he had captured the uncertain favour of the least royal of kings by flattering his weaknesses and serving his prejudices. He had dreamed of subduing nature to the service of man ; as yet he had succeeded only in shadowing forth the plan of his campaign.

But the supreme tragic possibility of his career was averted ; he was not content. He knew that his true work was still to be done.

Sir Sidney Lee writes : " Bacon deliberately chose the worser way. He abandoned in practice the last shreds of his political principles ; he gave up all hope of bringing about an accommodation on lines of right and justice between the King and the people. He made up his mind to remain a servant of the Crown, with the single and unpraiseworthy end of benefiting his own pocket." This is not even just to Bacon, whose career deserves some pity as well as justice. The mean, selfish motives of his obsequiousness to James cannot be denied ; but with them were mingled high motives. Bacon believed that the abuse of royal power was a less evil than the subjection of the royal power to the will of the people. He despised and distrusted the people ; he believed in the divine right of the King. His ideal was government by the King in conference with the best councillors—especially with Francis Bacon ; but if the King refused the best advice, Bacon probably felt that duty both to King and State obliged him to make the best of whatever action the King actually proposed. If things were bad in spite of his efforts to restrain and modify and direct the King's schemes, they would have been worse if he had removed his influence altogether. Possibly a greater statesman might have been strong enough to dominate James ; but Bacon's failure to do that does not constitute " deliberate choice of the worser way." And in the strange, many-coloured web of Bacon's motives, inseparably interwoven with the tarnished shreds of selfish desire for place and wealth and power, shines undimmed and unbroken the golden thread of his noble philosophical ambition : to lead men " to approach with humility and veneration to unroll the volume of Creation, to linger and meditate therein, and with minds washed clean from opinions to study it in purity and integrity."

The story of the prosperous years which followed

Bacon's appointment to the Attorney-Generalship may
be told very briefly. It sheds no new light on his
character, but adds fresh evidence of good and bad
qualities alike. In matters where his judgment and
action were untrammelled by consideration of James
and his favourites, Bacon filled his new office most
worthily. With the King's support, he continued his
attack on duelling. He prepared a " proposition," unluckily not accepted, for the reform of the laws, tending
consistently to simplicity and practical utility. In
political matters, he steadily supported James in his
assertion of his prerogative, but advised tactful treatment of Parliament, and compromise on non-essentials.
The claim which his usefulness gained on the King's
confidence he safeguarded and strengthened by careful
conciliation of the favourites. He bribed and flattered
the infamous Somerset. When the brighter star of
Villiers arose, he offered homage in terms which recall
those inspired by his early hopes from Essex.

As with Essex, as for a brief time with James, so now
with Villiers, Bacon's longing for a worthy patron seems
to have blinded his judgment. The rapid and unchecked
rise of Villiers from title to title, until as Duke of
Buckingham he was the greatest power in the State, may
well have captured Bacon's imagination ; and he lost no
time in attaching himself to the man who swayed the
King. Buckingham, on his side, felt enough admiration
for Bacon to value his flattery, though not enough, as
Bacon soon found, to listen patiently to his advice.
Fortune seemed now to play into Bacon's hands. He
was named to the Privy Council. He saw his old enemy
Coke disgraced and dismissed for resistance, at once
arrogant and courageous, to a royal mandate trenching
on the privileges of the Court of the King's Bench. In
March 1617, by Buckingham's influence, he was pro-
moted to the highest legal office, the Lord Keepership
of the Great Seal ; thus at last he gained his father's
office and official residence, succeeding to his birthplace,
and to the birthright of his powers.

Bacon once again amply justified his promotion. His

speech on first taking his seat in Chancery proclaimed
a new order of the administration of justice, strict,
impartial, responsible, and prompt. Later we shall
discuss his breaches of the rules he laid down for himself ; here it must simply be recorded that he followed
customs which he himself condemned : he accepted
money from suitors, he did not venture to protest
when Buckingham wrote to him to influence his judgments. Even in these respects he was better than most
of his predecessors, though far below his own ideal.
In sense of responsibility and willingness to give judgment on cases which a weaker man would have shirked,
and above all in indefatigable energy, he excelled
all his predecessors. He recognized alike the cost
and vexation of delay, and the dangers of hurried judgment, and met both evils by lengthening his day's
session and his term. By this means he wiped off in a
single month the very considerable arrears of cases which
had accumulated during his predecessor's illness ; and
only once was his judgment reversed.

But good work was no guarantee of continued pros-
perity ; Bacon held his office subject to the power by
which he had gained it—the favour of Buckingham.
Once he so far forgot his dependence as to urge unwelcome advice on his patron, and to act in its spirit.
The circumstances are particularly interesting. Bacon's
old enemy, Coke, scheming to regain place, recognized
the supreme importance of gaining Buckingham's support. To buy it he consented to his daughter's marriage
to the favourite's worthless brother, Sir John Villiers,
and agreed, far more unwillingly, to pay over a handsome dowry. His wife, the Lady Hatton whom Bacon
had once wooed, objected to the match ; and being a
lady of extremely independent will, secluded the girl.
Coke found his daughter's hiding place, and with his
sons and servants attacked it, broke in and carried her
off. Lady Hatton appealed to Bacon for help. He
did not know that Buckingham was particularly interested, and that the King approved of the match.
His instinct was naturally to take the side against

Coke, and political considerations and respect for order justified him. Accordingly he wrote to Buckingham, very strongly urging the abandonment of the match. Buckingham, who expected unquestioning support in return for his favours, was furious ; and the King himself wrote sharply rebuking Bacon. In fear of losing his office and stultifying his hopes in the moment of their fulfilment, Bacon made abject submission ; and when Buckingham accepted his apologies and mollified James's anger, he grovelled in professions of grateful devotion which offend against the merest decency of manhood :

" My ever best Lord, now better than Yourself,—Your lordship's pen, or rather pencil, hath pourtrayed towards me such magnanimity and nobleness and true kindness, as methinketh I see the image of some ancient virtue, and not anything of these times. It is the line of my life and not the lines of my letter, that must express my thankfulness ; wherein if I fail them, God fail me, and make me as miserable as I think myself at this time happy by this reviver, through his Majesty's singular clemency and your incomparable love and favour. . . ."

To write thus was to sign away all independence for the time of Buckingham's supremacy. Henceforth Bacon appears to have done unprotestingly the dirty work required of him. After the miserable tragedy of Raleigh's execution, he drew up a " Declaration of the Treasons of Sir Walter Raleigh," in which, as in the declaration of the treasons of Essex, his sense of the sanctity of law and order doubtless helped less worthy motives to put the worst interpretation on rash actions of a great man dead. Popular opinion did not forget the former case in reviling Bacon for the second. He served Buckingham, without perverting justice, in the trial and condemnation of the Earl and Countess of Suffolk. In the prosecution of the Attorney-General, Yelverton, he served Buckingham at the cost of loyalty to a true friend. When the question of patents of monopoly (by many of which Buckingham benefited) again became urgent, he did not entirely abandon his earlier attitude; and either from principle or policy supported the abolition of the most flagrant mono-polies. But he hastened to cringe to Buckingham, writing that he had spoken "somewhat like Ovid's mistress that strove, but yet as one that would be overcomen." Services such as these gained the reward not to be won by statesmanship or learning. Three months after his submission to Buckingham he received the full dignity of Lord Chancellor; in July 1618, he was raised to the peerage as Baron Verulam, and in January 1621, received the title of Viscount St. Albans.

It is painful to chronicle the degradation of a great man; with relief we turn to the other direction of Bacon's activity. While the politician was serving the King and his favourites, and securing at last the outward and temporary symbols of honour, the philosopher was still labouring for his dearer sovereign Knowledge, and establishing his title to enduring honour. In 1612 appeared a new, enlarged edition of the *Essays*. In 1620, after some twelve years' labour, he published the *Novum Organum*—the "new instrument" for the ad-vancement of learning and the conquest of nature—his most important philosophical work.

CHAPTER IV

BACON AND JAMES I. : THE DAYS OF ADVERSITY

BENEATH all the particular causes of dispute between James and his Parliaments lay a fundamental difference in principle. James believed in his divine right, and claimed to govern entirely according to his own will. He regarded every concession as a matter of favour or convenience. Parliament, on the contrary, asserted with increasing vigour its right to legislate for the needs of the State, and refused to recognize the royal prerogative as above the law. Under Elizabeth the struggle had been restrained by external dangers, by Elizabeth's

personal popularity, and by her acute political sense,
which led her to grant as graces those concessions which
Parliament regarded as essential and seemed disposed
if necessary to force from her. Now no urgent external
danger threatened; James was personally unpopular,
and singularly devoid of political sense. He stirred
up opposition by his prating arrogance, then taught
it its own power by his shiftiness and weakness.
For as long as possible, Bacon tried to harmonize the
assumptions of the King and the demands of Parliament. When it became impossible, he threw in his
lot with the King, not merely from interest, but from
his royalist principles. The long struggle had begun,
which was to end in the armed rebellion of Parliament
against the King, a rebellion which would have shocked
Bacon's deepest political feelings. His wisdom might
have moderated or even averted the final conflict, but
his advice was ignored. Thus, half from conviction,
half from necessity, he acted as agent of a policy which
provoked its own ruin; and he fell first victim to the
forces which later attacked Buckingham and at last
brought a king to the block.

The Parliament which met in January 1621 was not
hostile to Bacon personally. Its chief immediate
grievances were the extravagance of the King and
the evils consequent on favouritism; and amongst
these evils the most prominent was again the abuse
of monopolies, unjustly granted and oppressively enforced. The rascally extortions of Buckingham's
creatures, Michell and Mompesson, drew attention to
the whole system, and roused feeling too strong to be
satisfied by the punishment of these two minor rogues.
Buckingham, the real source of offence, evaded attack
by professing zeal for the proposed reforms. As scape-
goats remained the referees who sanctioned the patents,
of whom Bacon was the most important. The attack
upon them was urged by Coke, now the chief power in
the Commons, and by Sir Lionel Cranfield, a self-made
tradesman who had risen to be Master of the Wards,
and had gained considerable influence as champion of

economy. Coke's temperamental antipathy for Bacon
had been heightened by several disputes before the
game turned in Bacon's favour ; Bacon's share in his
discharge from the Chief Justiceship had kindled it
into hatred. Cranfield, as Master of the Wards, had
come into conflict with Bacon over the jurisdiction of
their respective Courts, and Bacon's unconcealed contempt had made of him another bitter enemy. Among
the Lords the need for reform was urged by another
enemy of Bacon, Southampton, who had not forgotten
Bacon's share in Essex's death and his own imprisonment. The reformers justly attacked the referees, and
raised such strong feeling against them, among the Lords
as well as the Commons, that James finally followed
Buckingham's lead, and disclaimed all responsibility
for their action. But Coke, Cranfield and Southampton
saw the opportunity of satisfying private vengeance
while serving public justice. Their reforming purpose
could well be served by bringing to book the most important offender ; and it suited Buckingham and James
admirably that attention should be diverted from the
general question to the sins of the Chancellor.

Bacon had seen the matter narrowing down to a legal
issue, on which, with the King's support in defence of
the royal prerogative, he might hope to baffle his
enemies. "Modicæ fidei quare dubitasti ?—Why didst
thou fear, O thou of little faith ? " he wrote to his friend
Matthew in March. But the direct danger was the
least ; indirectly the discredit thrown on him by the
inquiry into monopolies laid him open to a more deadly
attack. In February, the Commons in their reforming
zeal had appointed, as well as the committee on grievances
which had raised the question of monopolies, a committee
to inquire into abuses in the Courts of Justice. Confident in his efforts for reform and as yet not suspecting
any personal attack, Bacon had welcomed the inquiry,
" willingly consenting that any man might speak anything of his Court." Some abuses still remaining were
brought to light, and Churchill, a Chancery official who
had been discharged for extortion, volunteered adverse

evidence. As it grew clear that in the matter of monopolies Bacon was to be the scapegoat of the referees,
dissatisfied suitors began to venture personal charges
against him as a judge. On March 14th one Aubrey
accused him of accepting a bribe. Instantly he saw
his danger, though he still had no suspicion of its extent.
He recognized that an attack was intended against him
as an individual ; and though probably his profession
of conscious integrity was sincere, he knew that some
ugly evidence could be collected against him. " Your
Lordship spoke of Purgatory," he wrote to Buckingham
that same day. " I am now in it, but my mind is in a
calm ; for my fortune is not my felicity. I know I
have clean hands and a clean heart. . . . But Job himself, or whosoever was the justest judge, by such hunting for matters against him as hath been used against
me, may for a time seem foul, specially in a time when
greatness is the mark, and accusation is the game."

Other similar charges followed Aubrey's, and the
Commons invited an inquiry by the Lords. Bacon,
too ill to appear in his place, begged for time to answer
his accusers and for the opportunity of cross-examining
witnesses. It was ominous that their non-committal
reply was moved by his enemy Southampton. The
Lords appointed three committees to examine witnesses,
thus becoming prosecutors in the case they were to
judge.

Bacon withdrew to Gorhambury, where he lived in
all his usual pomp, and preserved the appearance of
confidence ; but his nerve was shaken by ill-health and
anxiety. On April 10th he drafted his will ; the famous
opening words show how in this bitter hour, when his
countrymen stood against him, and pomp seemed an
empty mockery, his confidence in his greatness remained
firm : " I bequeath my soul to God alive, by the obla-
tion of my Saviour. My body to be buried obscurely.
My name to the next age and to foreign nations." The
same mixture of sincere if limited religious feeling and
of self-justification appears in the prayer which he
wrote at this time—rather a stately apology and defence

than a prayer—confessing in general terms his weaknesses, confidently professing his good deeds, and accepting with dignity the chastisements of adversity.

During the days before the definite statement of the charges against him, Bacon considered his defence. He could not deny that he had accepted bribes, but he did deny, probably truly, that he had ever perverted justice in consequence. Certainly in the three most prominent cases, he had decided against the suitor who had bribed him. Such action was entirely in accord with Bacon's character. No man ever strove more persistently, and with less sense of inconsistency, to serve God and Mammon. He cherished a high ideal of justice, and actually carried out many salutary reforms in its administration; but the temptation of profit sanctioned by custom was too strong for a nature which replaced a moral code by a utilitarian ethical system. Like most intellectual gymnasts, Bacon was an adept at climbing over, or wriggling under, an awkward moral fence; he could get to the other side of it, and yet be able to tell himself that he had not broken through. He profited by the bribe, and justice did not suffer; then the bribe became a mere gift, a perquisite which folly paid and wisdom pocketed and ignored. It is even possible that the moral difficulty simply did not exist for him. In a memorandum of considerations which he wished to lay before the King, he distinguishes between " bargain or contract for reward to pervert justice " and the acceptance of a bribe " when the cause is really ended." " For the first," he declares, " I take myself to be as innocent as any born upon St. Innocent's Day, in my heart. . . . For the last, I conceived it to be no fault."

On April 17th the committees presented a list of twenty-eight definite charges against him. The King would not or could not intervene, and Buckingham had already abandoned him in a convenient, sudden access of morality, as cynical as cowardly—" with so bad a case he could have no sympathy." In the subsequent proceedings, however, Buckingham had the grace to advocate the acceptance of his submission, and to vote against his sentence. When Bacon knew the details of the charges he abandoned hope of defence. Instead of standing the trial he had begged, and attempting to make out at least a case in extenuation, he attempted to avoid detail, confessed himself guilty on the general charge, and implored " a benign interpretation." Old hostilities told against him now. Coke kept up the fury of the Commons ; and when the House of Lords seemed wavering towards pity for one of its greatest members so fallen, the rigour of the law was invoked by Southampton, mindful of Essex's trial and his own, by Suffolk, whom Bacon had prosecuted for his frauds as Treasurer, and by Howard, Suffolk's son. His submission was refused ; he was forced to reply on each separate charge, and on May 3rd he was condemned.

" This High Court doth adjudge :

1. That the Lord Viscount St. Alban, Lord Chancellor of England, shall undergo fine and ransom of forty thousand pounds.
2. That he shall be imprisoned in the Tower during the King's pleasure.
3. That he shall for ever be incapable of an office, place or employment in the State or Commonwealth.
4. That he shall never sit in Parliament, nor come within the verge of Court."

Thus in the fulness of time the man who had declaimed justly and unmercifully against the crime of Essex suffered just and unmerciful sentence under circumstances dramatically resembling those under which Essex was condemned. Essex acted criminally, but without criminal intent ; Bacon himself had pressed for sentence on the deed, brushing aside the plea of extenuating circumstances, and urging the consequence to the State. Similarly, Bacon acted criminally without criminal intent ; his action had corrupted the springs of justice as Essex's action had threatened the foundation of the State, and no plea of inadvertence or ignorance could avail either. In both cases, though punishment was demanded by justice, it was ensured and accelerated and aggravated by the malice of personal enemies. In both cases the culprit acknowledged the justice of the sentence, though protesting innocence of the gravest charges on which it was passed.

Bacon's own summary of his case cannot be improved : " I was the justest judge that was in England these fifty years. But it was the justest censure in Parliament that was these two hundred years." The first sentence states the conviction which numbed Bacon's moral sense, and let him protest innocence until he learned the details of the charges against him. Because he knew that he was just, he did not recognize the evil effect on justice of his example. In the second sentence speaks the true reformer and patriot, whose ideal of the sanctity of justice had found noble expression— the tragic irony of it !—in advice to Buckingham. " Judges must be men of courage, fearing God and hating coveteousness ; an ignorant man cannot, a coward dares not be a good judge. By no means be you persuaded to interpose yourself by word or letter in any cause depending, or like to be depending, in any court of justice, nor suffer any man to do it when you can hinder it. . . . If it should prevail, it perverts justice ; but if the judge be so just, and of so undaunted courage (as he ought to be) as not to be inclined thereby, yet it always leaves a taint of suspicion and prejudice behind it. Judges must be chaste as Cæsar's wife, neither to be nor so much as suspected in the least degree unjust."

In this inconsistency in Bacon's own nature lies the chief explanation of his sudden abandonment of every effort to defend himself. The idealist suddenly saw the actions of the man of customary morality in their true light, and condemned himself before he was condemned by his peers. The reformer rejoiced in the triumph of his idea, though it was at the cost of his own fall. He illustrates his own theory that every living thing is driven by two forces, the desire for individual good and the desire for the good of the community ; and that, while the former is the more urgent at any given moment, the latter is stronger in its ultimate power. This spirit gave Bacon some comfort when his political hopes lay broken among the ruins of his career. Greatness and nobility speak in the opening words of his submission to the Lords : " In the midst of a state of as great affliction as mortal man can endure, honour being above life . . . I should begin with the professing gladness in some things. The first is that hereafter the greatness of a judge or magistrate shall be no sanctuary or protection of guiltiness, which is the beginning of the golden world. The next, that after this example it is like that judges will fly from anything that is in the likeness of corruption as from a serpent."

Some of Bacon's critics have found new matter for condemnation in this sudden submission, thinking it merely cowardly. It is true that other reasons must have mingled with his sense of guilt ; he may have felt that resistance would draw down a heavier punishment, and that self-abasement might mitigate it. When he had seen the detailed charges he could not doubt the issue ; he knew too well, from many prosecutions which he had himself conducted, that defence was useless before a hostile tribunal. Trial might have elicited some facts in his favour, but it would also have advertised the particulars of his shame. Pride might have urged a stronger or a worse man to fight, though convinced of his guilt ; Bacon's pride was turned to shame in its inmost sources by self-condemnation.

The sentence was not enforced in its severity. The fine was remitted by assignment to trustees ; the " imprisonment in the Tower during the King's pleasure " was satisfied by a few dreadful days ; and after two years of pitiful and persistent entreaty, Bacon gained readmission to " the verge of court "—that is, permission to live in London—and general pardon. In payment for these last favours, Buckingham, with incredible meanness, forced from him the gift of York House, the home to which he clung with more sentiment than he showed in any other connection : " York House is the house where my father died and where I first

breathed, and there will I yield my last breath, if it so
please God, and the King will give me leave."

As soon as Bacon had recovered from the first shock
of his disgrace he began to drag himself again towards
the foot of the ladder which in forty long years he had
climbed so toilfully, only to be hurled down. No
catastrophe could destroy his instinct to climb, or his
passion to serve the State as an administrator. Repeatedly he had acknowledged that he was " fitter to
hold a book than play a part," " fitted for nothing so well
as the study of Truth " ; repeatedly he had lamented
" multum incola fuit anima mea,"—" my soul hath
been a stranger in the course of her pilgrimage." Now
he could scarcely hope for office high enough to enable
him to " gain commandment of more wits than a man's
own " for his vast contemplative ends ; and all his experience proved that even the highest office, in his
day and under his King, added little to his power of
serving knowledge indirectly, while its duties took the
time that might have been given to direct personal
service. Still to cling to the old dream proved an
essential passion for State employment which might
wear the livery of his other passion, but which indeed
was stuff of his very being. In the wonderful age of
which he was one of the latest true sons, when every
limitation chafed the giant spirit thirsting for every
source of experience, tingling with the desire of conscious
strength to exercise itself in every kind of activity,
nobly eager to serve fully as well as ambitious to gain
the whole treasure of living, even the greatest thinker
could not be content with a life of meditation ; even to
found philosophy anew seemed an achievement inadequate to a man's whole powers. As a philosopher
Bacon declared that the life of action is worthier than
the life of meditation, and he shaped his life in accord-
ance with this belief.

There is thus no reason for surprise, though much for
pity and regret, in Bacon's unwearied efforts to re-enter
the servitude from which he had been flung. He had
longed all through life for an opportunity to serve

truth diligently ; an angel with a flaming sword drove
him into his Eden, and he languished for the curse of
his old labour. He addressed appeals at once sincere
and diplomatic, pitiful in their urgency and admirable
in their eloquence, to the King, to Buckingham, to
every friend, even to enemies like his ungenerous
successor Bishop Williams and his enemy Cranfield,
wherever there seemed hope of serving his purpose.
It was all vain ; even the change in monarch, even the
lapse of time which had served Suffolk, and which
served the Somersets and Bacon's guiltier fellow-
culprit Bennett, brought no new opportunity for Bacon.
He never again held even the smallest office ; he was
never again admitted to Parliament ; his uninvited
memoranda of advice on State affairs were ignored.

But though discouraged in offers of service and
weakened by frequent illness, he could not be idle.
" It is counted a great bliss for a man to have Leisure
with Honour. That was never my fortune. For time
was, I had the Honour without Leisure ; and now I
have Leisure without Honour. . . . But my desire is
now to have Leisure without Loitering, and . . . to
yield some fruit of my private life." With these words
he sent to Elizabeth of Bohemia a copy of his *History
of Henry VII*, the first fruits of his new labours, completed in October 1621, and published in the following
March. In 1622, turning from " the City " to " the
Temple," he wrote in dialogue form the (unfinished)
Advertisement touching a Holy War, advocating the
Spanish marriage as leading to joint action of Spain
and England against the Turk. To his historical work he
added the fragment of a *History of Henry VIII*—one
morning's work. He worked on the *Digest of the Laws*
which he had offered to James. " For recreation in
my sickness," as he wrote in the preface, he
made the collection of *Apophthegms New and Old*
published in 1624 (dated 1625) ; evidence of his
astonishing memory, for, says Rawley, " this collection
his Lordship made out of his memory without turning
any book." The *Translation of certain Psalms into*

English Verse, written during illness in 1624, and published in 1625 with a dedication to his " very good friend, Mr. George Herbert," deserves mention only as final proof, for those perverse enough to need it, that Bacon could not conceivably have written any of Shakespeare's verse. Above all he laboured at the third section of his " great instauration " of philosophy, collecting the materials in natural history upon which, by his method, a new natural philosophy was to be based. In November 1622 appeared the first part of this section, dealing with the phenomena of winds (usually cited as *Historia Naturalis*). In the following January appeared the " Account of Life and Death " (*Historia vitæ et mortis*).

While thus proceeding with the laborious detailed work of the third section, he recast and greatly added to the *Advancement of Learning,* that eloquent survey of the purpose and method of his whole work, and published it in Latin in 1623, as the first volume of his collected works : *Opera F. Baconis de Verulamio . . . tomus primus qui continet de Dignitate et Augmentis Scientiarum libros IX.* (usually cited as *De Augmentis*). In these years, too, returning to a conception which had long attracted him, he wrote the unfinished sketch of the *New Atlantis,* his ideal State, the home of knowledge. A " newly enlarged " edition of his Essays in 1625, adding nineteen new essays to the edition of 1612, was the last of his works published during his lifetime. Other works of these last years, but none of first-rate importance, were published after his death.

Bacon's last days were spent in a record of experiments and alleged facts in natural history, *Sylva Sylvarum* ;[1] and experiment was the cause of his death.

[1] The title has been called obscure, but it would be comprehensible to contemporaries. We may quote from Ben Jonson's exposition of the term *sylva,* which he used as title for his collection of thoughts on men, morals, literature and life. " As we are commonly used to call the infinite mixed multitude of growing trees a wood, so the ancients gave the name of Sylvæ— Timber Trees—to books of theirs in which small works of various and diverse matter were promiscuously brought together " (Morley's translation). Bacon's book presented not only the

The circumstances may fittingly be told in the words of the next great English philosopher, Hobbes, who knew him well during his last years.

"The cause of his Lordship's death was trying an experiment. As he was taking an air in a coach with Dr. Witherborne (a Scotchman, physician to the King) towards Highgate, snow lay on the ground, and it came into my Lord's thoughts, why flesh might not be preserved in snow as in salt. They alighted out of the coach, and went into a poor woman's house at the bottom of Highgate Hill, and bought a hen, and made the woman exenterate it, and then stuffed the body with snow, and my Lord did help to do it himself. The snow so chilled him, that he immediately fell so extremely ill, that he could not return to his lodgings (at Gray's Inn), but went to the Earl of Arundel's house at Highgate, where they put him into a good bed warmed with a pan, but it was a damp bed that had not been lain in about a year before, which gave him such a cold that in two or three days he died of suffocation."

"The experiment succeeded excellently well," he told his absent host, Lord Arundel, in a letter apologising for his sudden compulsory visit. It was the first experiment in refrigeration. It made one step towards that conquest of Nature by knowledge which was Bacon's dream. So his life ended in humble and faithful service of knowledge, fulfilling his own precept: "This should men study to be perfect in, and becoming again as little children condescend to take the alphabet of it into their hands, and spare no pains to search and unravel the interpretation thereof, but pursue it strenuously and persevere even unto death."

"wood" of his own observations and experiments, but material collected from other men's "woods." He offered a "review of reviews," a "collection of collections," a "wood of woods."

CHAPTER V

BACON'S PHILOSOPHY

The sovereignty of man lieth hid in knowledge. Now we govern nature in opinions, but we are thrall unto her in necessity ; but if we could be led by her in invention, we should command her in action."—*Praise of Knowledge.*

A BRIEF statement of Bacon's philosophy cannot attempt treatment of his works individually. The same ideas often reappear (sometimes with some inconsistency in their expression), and the same purposes and principles inform all he wrote, formal treatise or essay or occasional fragment. The philosophical works may therefore best be treated as a whole ; but it is convenient first to state the particular position of each volume in the general scheme of the *Great Instauration.* The *Advancement of Learning* (1605) and its mature, developed version, the *De Augmentis* (1623) stand somewhat apart. They set forth the need for, and the potentialities of, a new philosophy, and criticize accepted views and methods ; they proclaim the importance of learning, exhibiting knowledge as the hope of mankind, and indicate the direction in which it must turn in order truly to serve mankind. The *Advancement* was intended, says Bacon, in a simile which he often repeated and varied, " but as an image in a cross-way, that may point out the way, but cannot go it." Its later form, *De Augmentis,* he brought into nearer though not integral connection with the *Instauration ;* " for that my book of Advancement of Learning may be some preparative, or key, for the better opening of the Instauration ; because it exhibits a mixture of new conceits and old ; whereas the Instauration gives the new unmixed, otherwise than with some little aspersion of the old for taste's sake ; I have thought good to procure a translation of that book into the general language, not without great and ample additions and enrichment thereof, especially in the second book, which handleth the Partition of Sciences ; in such sort, as I hold it may serve in lieu of the first part of the Instauration, and acquit my promise in that part."

The second part of the *Instauration*, according to the plan prefixed to the *Novum Organum*, was to deal with the proper method of interpreting Nature, which seemed to Bacon the most important work of all. This section is represented by the *Novum Organum, or Indications concerning the Interpretation of Nature* (1620), the most important expression of Bacon's fundamental principles. Here are included in their most mature form many thoughts stated in the earlier miscellanies—*Temporis Partus Maximus, Valerius Terminus, Cogitata et Visa, Filum Labyrinthi* and minor fragments.

The third part was to collect material for treatment according to the new method : *Phœnomena Universi, or a Natural and Experimental History for the Construction of Philosophy.* On this he laboured in his last years. The fourth section, *Scala Intellectus, the Ladder of the Intellect,* was to record results obtained by the new method ; and the fifth, *Prodromi, the Forerunners, or Anticipations of the New Philosophy,* was similarly to record his observations independent of the new method. Towards these collections Bacon produced no more than prefaces, a few fragments, and incidental passages under other heads. The sixth and final section he never hoped to complete. It was to embody the new philosophy itself—*Philosophia Secunda, or Active Science,* the knowledge ultimately to be gained when the new method had been applied to all the phenomena of the universe. This section " placed beyond our power and beyond our hope," Bacon bequeathed, like his fame, to posterity.

Perhaps no great man has suffered so much from superficial and prejudiced criticism as Bacon ; and it is particularly unfortunate that so many of those who can claim merely a bowing acquaintance with his work have been introduced to it by Macaulay. That eloquent apostle of the obvious proclaimed only half the truth alike of his character and of his philosophical purpose and achievement. It is true that Bacon's immediate philosophical purpose was practical. He sought to propagate " man's empire over the universe." But that was not all ; his service of knowledge was to serve mankind more loftily than by the mere conquest of necessities. He saw in knowledge the interpreter of God's purposes.[1] To justify the ways of God to men it was only necessary to free men's sight from the baffling films of ignorance and misapprehension, so that they might see the true nature of the works of God. " We copy the sin of our first parents while we suffer for it. They wished to be like God, but their posterity wish to be even greater. . . . For we will have it that all things· *are* as in our folly we think they should be, not as seems fittest to the Divine Wisdom, or as they are found to be in fact. . . . We clearly impress the stamp of our own image on the creatures and works of God, instead of carefully examining and recognizing in them the stamp of the Creator himself. . . . If, therefore, there be any humility toward the Creator, any reverence for or disposition to magnify his works, any charity for man and anxiety to relieve his sorrows and necessities, any love of truth in nature, any desire for the purification of the understanding, we must entreat men again and again to discard, or at least to set apart for a while, these volatile and preposterous philosophies which have preferred theses to hypotheses, led experience captive, and triumphed over the works of God ; and to approach with humility and veneration to unroll the volume of Creation, to linger and meditate therein, and with minds washed clean from opinions to study it in purity and integrity." [2]

Two great conscious purposes thus directed Bacon's

[1] Bacon repeatedly declares that the " natural evidences," by which knowledge may prove God's existence, power and goodness, in no way trespass on the mysteries of faith, which lie entirely beyond the province of reason. Religion and Philosophy, he says, alike suffer from being "commixed together."

[2] Preface to *Historia Naturalis*, Spedding's translation.

philosophy : the service of the practical needs of man, and the service of the highest in man's intellect by discovery of the true nature of God's works. Both purposes demanded the same method. of labour: obedience to nature (*natura parendo vincitur*), careful establishment of the exact facts of natural phenomena, the penetration to the essential beneath the apparent. The execution of the whole task lay beyond the power of any one man ; Bacon set himself only to proclaim the method which all should use : " I hold it enough to have constructed the machine though I may not succeed in setting it on work."

But a force even stronger than the most utilitarian or the most idealistic of conscious purposes drove him to work and inspired his method : an inborn passion for truth, an insatiable hunger for knowledge. " For myself, I found that I was fitted for nothing so well as for the study of Truth ; as having a mind nimble and versatile enough to catch the resemblances of things (which is the chief point), and at the same time steady enough to fix and distinguish their subtler differences ; as being gifted by nature with desire to seek, patience to doubt, fondness to meditate, slowness to assert, readiness to reconsider, carefulness to dispose and set in order ; and as being a man that neither affects what is new nor admires what is old, and that hates every kind of imposture. So I thought my nature had a kind of familiarity and relationship with Truth. . . . I am not hunting for fame : I have no desire to found a sect, and to look for any private gain from such an undertaking as this, I count both ridiculous and base. Enough for me the consciousness of well-deserving, and those real and effectual results with which fortune itself cannot interfere." [1]

According to Rawley, Bacon was dissatisfied, even as an undergraduate, with the Aristotelian teaching.[2] His quarrel was really less with Aristotle than with the scholasticism which claimed him as its supreme

---

[1] *De Interpretatione Naturæ Proœmium*, Spedding's translation.
[2] *V.s.*, p. 10.

authority. " Surely, like as many substances in nature
which are solid, do putrefy and corrupt into worms ;
so it is the property of good and sound knowledge
to putrefy and dissolve into a number of subtle, idle,
unwholesome, and (as I may term them) vermiculate
questions, which have indeed a kind of quickness of life
and spirit, but no soundness of matter or goodness of
quality. This kind of degenerate learning did chiefly
reign amongst the schoolmen : who having strong and
sharp wits, and abundance of leisure, and small variety
of reading, but their wits being shut up in the cells of
a few authors (chiefly Aristotle their dictator) as their
persons were shut up in the cells of monasteries and
colleges, and knowing little history, either of nature or
time, did out of no great quantity of matter and infinite
agitation of wit spin out unto us those laborious webs of
learning which are extant in their books. For the wit
and mind of man, if it work upon matter, which is the
contemplation of the creatures of God, worketh according to the stuff and is limited thereby ; but if it
work upon itself, as the spider worketh his web, then it
is endless, and brings forth indeed cobwebs of learning,
admirable for the fineness of thread and work but of
no substance or profit." [1]

His contempt for the " unprofitable subtility " of
the schoolmen leads him to look with disfavour upon
their traditional authorities ; but, though he attacks
Greek philosophers without much discrimination in the
Redargutio, he does not escape their influence. (Naturally it is to Plato that he owes most—the chosen
philosopher of the Renascence, as Aristotle was of the
Middle Ages.) He admits their honesty of purpose
and the importance of their goal ; it is their method
that he challenges : " the question between me and the
ancients is not of the virtue of the race, but of the
rightness of the way." Alike in ancient and in mediæval
philosophy, deductive methods have led men far away
from facts into vain imaginings. On the other hand
the mechanical arts, which are based upon experience,

[1] *Advancement of Learning,* Book I. iv. 5.

have made great progress. By their method, the inductive, learning could be given a new, firm foundation. Purposeful experiment and observation must replace blind theorizing.

The *method* is to be inductive, ascending to general axiom from carefully established facts. The *material* upon which it is to work includes all the phenomena of the universe. Bacon complains that there has been too much specialization. True knowledge must take account of all types of phenomena, must recognize that all branches of learning spring from one trunk; or, to use another metaphor, men must ascend from the plains of special studies, where the view is limited, to the hilltop of general fundamental principles, from which the whole province of knowledge may be surveyed. Accordingly he declares " I have taken all knowledge for my province." In the *Advancement of Learning*, for the convenience of systematic treatment, he maps out the ground.

First, *divine learning* must be separated from *human learning;* in the former, reason is merely the handmaid of faith; it can furnish " natural evidences " of the existence and power and wisdom of God, but it cannot disclose His nature; it can supplement revelation in practical questions of Church government, but revelation alone can teach the mysteries of faith and the highest moral law. Human learning Bacon divides, according as the function exercised is memory, imagination or reason (not a satisfactory basis), into *History*, *Poesy*, and *Philosophy*. History records the facts of nature (natural history) or of various directions of human activity (civil, ecclesiastical, and literary history). Under Poesy he includes all imaginative work whether in prose or verse. It is " nothing else but feigned history." He allows that " poesy serveth and conferreth to magnanimity, morality, and delectation," but regards it chiefly as a popular forerunner of learning, and a useful aid to the historian and the orator. " It is not good to stay too long in the theatre." His threefold division of poesy into narrative, representative and allusive, is not satisfactory from any point of view. He seems to prefer the "allusive or parabolical"—that is, didactic narrative, especially allegory. (We recommend this preference to the notice of supporters of the Bacon-Shakespeare theory.) He misses the true value of poetry in exercising and developing the imagination; he does not recognize that, in Shelley's words, "the great instrument of moral good is the imagination; . . . poetry strengthens the faculty which is the organ of the moral nature of man." He does not even grasp the true distinction between poetic and historic truth, though Sidney, in a charming passage of the *Apology for Poetry*, had reminded its antagonists of Aristotle's famous judgment that "poetry is a more philosophical and a higher thing than history: for poetry tends to express the universal, history the particular."

The third division, Philosophy, is the most important to Bacon. Again he distinguishes three branches, according to the object contemplated. "In philosophy the contemplations of man do either penetrate unto God, or are circumferred to nature, or are reflected or reverted upon himself. Out of which several inquiries there do arise three knowledges, Divine philosophy, Natural philosophy, and Human philosophy or Humanity. For all things are marked and stamped with this triple character, of the power of God, the difference of nature, and the use of man." All these must be approached by "a main and common way," "one universal science, . . . primitive or summary philosophy," though later they diverge as branches spread from a common stem.

Divine philosophy he dismisses in two brief but eloquent paragraphs. "The bounds of this knowledge are, that it sufficeth to convince atheism, but not to inform religion."

Natural philosophy falls under two heads: "the inquisition of causes, and the production of effects; speculative and operative; natural science and natural prudence." These are closely connected, but need separate treatment "because all true and fruitful natural philosophy hath a double scale or ladder, . . .

ascending from experiments to the invention of causes, and descending from causes to the invention of new experiments." *Natural science* he divides into *Physic* and *Metaphysic*, carefully explaining that he uses the latter term in a new sense, applying it, like Physic, to natural objects : " Physic should contemplate that which is inherent in matter, and therefore transitory ; and Metaphysic that which is abstract and fixed. . . . Physic handleth the material and efficient causes ; Metaphysic the formal and final causes." Here the *Advancement* anticipates the doctrine of essential " forms " in things, determining their properties yet distinct from them, later developed in the *Novum Organum ;* to this we shall return. Under *Metaphysic* he includes mathematics. The most interesting point in the subdivision of *Natural Prudence* is that he gives the third place, after " experimental " and " philosophical " sections, to " magical conceits " ; dismissing " credulous and superstitious conceits " but acknowledging " true natural magic, which is that great liberty and latitude of operation which dependeth upon the knowledge of forms." " Magic " is thus the practical application of " metaphysic," dealing with objects according to their hidden ultimate properties instead of according to their properties as directly perceived. The Renascence instinct for the infinite catches alike at mediæval mystic doctrine and the " idea " teaching of Plato. Here, for an instant, Bacon strangely touches hands with Paracelsus.

Human philosophy Bacon divides according as its object is the individual or society. He distinguishes, in the former, between the science dealing with the body, and that dealing with the mind. The latter includes both psychology and ethics, but the distinction is not closely observed, and in neither section are the subdivisions exhaustive. The science of the body is still more loosely subdivided into " Medicine, Cosmetic, Athletic, Sensual Arts." In the first and most important subsection he notices particularly the gaps in contemporary knowledge of anatomy.

This detailed survey of the field of knowledge discovers deficiencies and errors in every part. To supply and correct these, to gain the insight into nature's order which constitutes both knowledge and power, the philosopher must observe three conditions : he must criticize and correct his own perceptions, conceptions, inferences ; he must draw his material from experience, and here systematic experiment and observation are needed, not mere reference to a chaos of facts ; and he must not generalize rashly, but must proceed step by step from the particular statement of fact, based on experience, to the general principle.

The philosopher is bound, in his observations, to use his senses ; in his reasoning, to use his intellect. His first step, therefore, must be to ensure that sense and intellect do their work perfectly. Through both error may creep into the result. The senses are imperfect instruments. The eye, for example, fails to observe bodies extremely small, or in very swift motion, or obscured by other bodies. None of the senses is capable of furnishing exact and full information about physical properties. They therefore need the aid of apparatus.

Still more dangerous are the inherent faults of the intellect ; and these Bacon discusses repeatedly. " Facility to believe, impatience to doubt, temerity to answer, glory to know, doubt to contradict, end to gain, sloth to search, seeking things in words, resting in part of nature ; these, and the like, have been the things which have forbidden the happy match between the mind of man and the nature of things, and in place thereof have married it to vain notions and blind experiments " (*Praise of Knowledge*). Some of the defects here named are mentioned again in the catalogue of "peccant humours" in the *Advancement*. In the *Delineatio* he lays down that the mind must be cleared of false ideas both borrowed and innate. These ideas are due to the imperfection of the mind, and at the same time constitute a new imperfection. If the mind were a perfect mirror it would reflect correct images ; but, since it is uneven, or "like an enchanted glass [*i.e.* a distorting

mirror] full of superstition and imposture" it gives
false reflections. These false reflections Bacon calls
"idols of the mind," borrowing a Platonic term which
the *Novum Organum* later made classical in English. An
idol is first, the distorted image of an object in contrast
with the true image of its essential nature, the "divine
idea"[1] of it, which would be given by the "even
mirror" of a perfect understanding. In the *Novum
Organum*, where this doctrine of "idols" or "phantoms
of the mind" is developed with admirable acuteness
and originality, the term carries a further sense. The
"idol" is not merely the false reflection; it is also
that imperfection in the mirror which falsifies the reflection, that inherent defect of the mind which unfits it
to form correct images; it is a cause as well as an effect.

Of such tendencies to error inherent in the understanding, Bacon distinguishes four types : idols of the
tribe, of the cave or den, of the market-place, of the
theatre (idola tribus, specus, fori, theatri). "The idols
of the tribe have their foundation in human nature
itself, in the very tribe or race of men." Such are
above all the illusions of the senses; further, the
tendency to judge too hastily, to cling to agreeable
beliefs in spite of facts, and to give credit to affirmative rather than negative evidence; the anthropo-
morphic conception of the universe; and the associated
instinct to see purpose in the processes of nature (by
analogy with human action) instead of considering them
merely in the mechanical relation of cause and effect.
The remedy lies in objective treatment of phenomena;
the philosopher must not attempt to bring nature into
the narrow limit of the mind, by analogy, but must
extend his mind to grasp the realities of nature.

The "idols of the den" have their origin in the
peculiar constitution, mental or physical, of each individual, and also in education, habit and accident; "for

---

[1] Here he uses Plato's term *idea*, but not in Plato's sense of an
abstract shaping force. The *idea* is for Bacon the same thing as
the *form*—the essential nature of the thing itself, its fixed character
beneath shifting and misleading appearances.

every one (besides the faults he shares with his race) has a cave or den of his own, which refracts and discolours the light of nature." Here come into question the individual tendency of the mind to dwell predominantly (with the theologians) on resemblances, or (with the lawyers) on differences between things, instead of equally on both ; and the habits of thought imposed by profession—Aristotle treats the world as a syllogism, the chemists find in it only a laboratory, the physicist Gilbert sees it as a magnet. Such errors may in part be corrected by comparison with the views of others.

Most troublesome of all are the " idols of the market-place," which have their origin in language, the necessary medium of men's intercourse. In the *Advancement* Bacon attacks the "fantastical learning" of the schoolmen because it attached too much importance to its expression. " Here is the first distemper of learning, when men study words and not matter." In the *Novum Organum* his criticism goes much deeper. In the very nature of language lies a source of error. A word is merely a conventional symbol for some thing, either concrete or abstract. The symbol must serve many people, each of whom may have a different conception of the thing it represents ; and since the word is property of the multitude, these conceptions will often be inaccurate. The significance of a word is therefore vague ; it does not convey an exact and definite image of the thing it represents. Who can define the exact quality denoted severally by the words humid, heavy, dense, rare ; or the exact action denoted severally by the words generate, corrupt ? In some cases names are given even to things which do not exist; " of this kind are fortune, the *primum mobile*, planetary orbits, the element of fire, and similar fictions which have their origin in false and idle theories." The mind unconsciously accepts the word as a true symbol, and the errors of language are thus transferred to thought ; " for men believe that their reason governs words ; but it is also true that words react on the mind." The mind works with the false images given by words instead of with the true images gained by observation and experiment. Here the remedy is clear : put no trust in words ; get behind the word-symbol to the thing itself.

The "idols of the theatre" arise from the mistaken dogmas of false systems of philosophy, which are "but so many stage plays, representing worlds of their own creation after an unreal and scenic fashion." Once more the remedy lies in whole-hearted allegiance to experience.

To recognize these sources of error is already to combat them. And such difficulties are no ground for the abandonment of the task of philosophy : "the greatest obstacle to progress is that men despair and think things impossible." Even the old, mistaken methods have produced some results ; from the new method everything may be expected. Bacon believes that his method of investigation can be applied to all sciences ; he develops it in immediate application to the natural sciences. Here his aim is determined by the hypothesis that all the infinitely various phenomena of nature are due to varying combination of a small number of fixed elementary properties which he calls "simple natures" ; such "simple natures" are, for example, those of warmth, cold, weight, age, death. (The mixture of examples is consequent on Bacon's assumption that every property which cannot be analysed into simpler properties must be a "simple nature.") Each simple nature has its cause, its being and its law in its *form*. We must dwell for a moment on Bacon's conception of "forms," for it constitutes the chief difficulty in his system. The *Advancement* distinguishes "that which is abstract and fixed" in a property, from "that which is inherent in matter and therefore transitory" ; "the formal and final causes" from "the material and efficient causes." The former phrase of each of these pairs defines "form." The sensible effects of the simple nature are simply the manifestation of a cause ; that cause is the "form." Heat is a "simple nature" ; it is the manifestation of vibrations of a certain type ; these are the "form" of heat. Thus

Bacon identifies "form" and "law," meaning by "law" not a general expression of what happens, but the being of the phenomenon in its abstract expression. "The form of a thing is the very thing itself, and the thing differs from the form no otherwise than as the apparent differs from the real, or the external from the internal, or the thing in reference to man from the thing in reference to the universe."

But the form is not to be separated from the material; it consists in a grouping or motion of small material particles. The form of heat is a special kind of motion; the form of the quality "white" is a special arrangement of the particles of material.

The business of natural philosophy is to determine these "forms," limited in number, which cause all phenomena. Bacon believes that to know them will be to command nature; for by combining them, exactly knowing each, man will be able to produce whatever results he desires. The dream of the alchemist is trifling beside this stupendous and magnificent hope. It is true that in so far as Bacon seeks to subdue nature to men's needs, his philosophy is utilitarian; but on such a scale utilitarianism catches something of the grandeur and glamour of idealism.

The method of investigation prescribed by Bacon is systematic induction. The current inductive method, "by simple enumeration," merely collected instances in which the phenomenon under investigation occurred, without any attempt at selection, and generalized from these. Bacon demands first as full a table as possible of these "affirmative instances" (cf. Mill's "Method of Agreement"). By this must then be set a table of "negative instances," cases similar to those of the first list in as many respects as possible, but not exhibiting the phenomenon in question. Comparison of these tables (cf. Mill's "Joint Method of Agreement and Difference") cuts out many non-essential conditions, and limits the field of search for the necessary conditions which define the cause.

A third table ("of Comparison") must include the cases

in which the phenomenon is present in greater or less degree ; from this (*cf.* Mill's "Method of Concomitant Variations ") may be recognized the conditions which, varying with the phenomenon, must either cause it or be caused by it. At this point, though the inductive process is by no means complete, enough has been done to permit a "first vintage," a hypothetical explanation. As example Bacon takes heat, and, on evidence collected under these three tables, defines its "form" as "a motion, expansive, restrained, and striving amongst the smaller particles of bodies "—a remarkable anticipation of the modern theory of heat, despite some errors in the evidence on which Bacon bases it. A fourth table "of Exclusions "—impossible in the complete form as Bacon plans it—is to show all cases where the phenomenon occurs, and then to cut out in succession all the "natures which cannot be its cause."

The *Novum Organum* further names nine "helps to the understanding," to supplement the tables. Bacon works out only one, the "*Prerogatives of Instances*," "characteristic phenomena selected from the great miscellaneous mass . . . on account of some peculiarly forcible way in which they strike the reason" (Herschel). At this stage, further, the deductive method finds a place ; the investigator rises by induction from experiment to axiom, then from the axiom determines by deduction the most fruitful direction of new experiment. The chief fault of Bacon's method is that it does not provide for the due use of hypothesis ; it insists in all cases on a mechanical progress from fact to axiom of low degree of generalization, from this to axiom more general, and so step by step to the axiom of highest generalization. Science has been better served by applying the reason to the facts upon a certain basis of experiment ; thus forming a hypothesis which further experiment may modify or confirm. Bacon made the mistake of seeking an infallible method, which, if carefully used, would in time place the ordinary intellect on a level with the genius. He was driven by the fantastic excesses of his scientific predecessors to distrust even a legitimate use of the imagination.

Further, though he urged the correlation of all the sciences, he was guilty of strange ignorances and prejudices. He entirely failed to recognize the vast importance to natural science of mathematics. He clung obstinately to the Ptolemaic theory, that the earth was the centre of the universe, round which all else revolved, ignoring the discoveries by which Galileo and Kepler proved the correctness of the Copernican system. He paid no attention to such epoch-making work as Napier's invention of logarithms, Harvey's discovery of the circulation of the blood, Gilbert's researches in magnetism. He did not himself apply his principles methodically in any science, though he threw out some brilliant suggestions, including anticipations of the modern theories of light, of heat, of the atomic constitution of matter. Even his method was not entirely new; Gilbert, whom he attacked, had applied the inductive method before Bacon gave it formal statement. But when all these admissions have been made, Bacon still remains the greatest of the early servants of natural philosophy. He has been called " the father of natural philosophy " ; more truly he might be named its first great apostle. He systematized and popularized the experimental method. He devoted his magnificent imagination and his unmatched eloquence to the propagation of the new gospel. With the fervour and the optimism of true faith he prophesied to men of the promised land of knowledge, and led them forth to seek it. " The fortune of the human race will give the issue ; such an issue, it may be, as in the present condition of things, of the minds of men, cannot easily be conceived or imagined. For the object in view is not only the contemplative happiness, but the whole fortunes, and affairs, and powers, and works of men."

Bacon intended his method to apply to all branches of knowledge. He attempted its systematic exposition only in the case of natural philosophy, the second of the three great branches into which he divides philosophy. The first branch, which deals with man's reflections on God, received from him only cursory attention. A word must still be said about his contribution to the last branch, which deals with man " as shown and exhibited to himself."

In this section, Bacon's limitations as a philosopher appear very clearly. His mind is extraordinarily unmetaphysical; he persistently ignores the ultimate problems of existence. He never asks the questions, fundamental in natural philosophy as well as in this section on " human philosophy ": how do we know that mind or matter exists ? What *is* " mind " ? What *is* " matter " ? In what relation do they stand ? These problems are too abstract for Bacon ; he does not even recognize the need for the great work which Descartes was so soon to begin. He simply assumes the existence of both mind and matter, and also the distinction and the relation between them—that the one is the thinking power, that the other is entirely independent in its existence, yet furnishes objects which the thinking power can recognize. His contributions to psychology are unimportant, but he proclaims the need for inquiry into the nature and origin of the mental faculties.

His views on ethics, on the other hand, are interesting, and he presents them with some attempt at system in the *De Augmentis*. Here again he ignores the fundamental question of freedom of will ; he assumes that " the will is governed by right reason " and " spurred " by the passions. *Ethic* is the science of the will, as logic is that of the reason. As the reason is baffled by "idols," so the will is baffled by false images of good. The first business of the moral philosopher, the theoretical half of Ethic, is to seek the true nature of good— a duty neglected, says Bacon, by his predecessors. Everything is moved by two forces, the one aiming at individual good, the other at the good of the community of which the thing is a part ; the latter force, the instinct to serve the general good, is the nobler and also the stronger, both in inanimate things, and, still more clearly, in man.

Of the virtues, love is the greatest. We are most like God when we live in charity with men ; the mediæval saints who secluded themselves from men were therefore misguided. The active life is worthier than the contemplative life, because the former is the life for the general good ; contemplation is good only if it is intended to lead to active service. "In this theatre of man's life, it is reserved only for God and angels to be lookers-on." In this emphasis on the worth of active service of the communal good, Bacon points the way for most English moral philosophers.

The second half of *Ethic* is practical ; its business is to teach how our nature may be brought into harmony with the "image of good" discovered in the former half. Bacon blames his predecessors for their silence on this matter ; more has been done here, he says, by historians and poets than by philosophers. The emotions have power to sway the reason, because the conception of present good produces a stronger effect on the mind than that of future good ; hence reason needs the support of custom, exercise, habit, education, and other similar "receipts and regiments." Most important of these is "the electing and propounding unto a man's self good and virtuous ends of his life, such as may be in a reasonable sort within his compass to attain. For if these two things be supposed, that a man set before him honest and good ends, and again, that he be resolute, constant, and true unto them ; it will follow that he shall mould himself into all virtue at once."

Thus again he concludes that the greatest of all virtues is charity or "divine love," "which is excellently called the bond of perfection, because it comprehendeth and fasteneth all virtues together. . . . If a man's mind be truly inflamed with charity, it doth work him suddenly into greater perfection than all the doctrine of morality can do, which is but a sophist in comparison of the other. . . . All other excellencies, though they advance nature, yet they are subject to excess. Only charity admitteth no excess."

" All good moral philosophy," says Bacon, " is but a
handmaid of religion " ; ethical science must be supple-
mented by revelation. Once more he ignores a fundamental question : what makes an action right ? That
inquiry, and the foundation in England of a scientific
system of ethics, remained for his great successor
Hobbes. Nor is Bacon concerned to inquire into the
nature of revelation. His standpoint is that of the
orthodox Christianity of his day ; and his statement
of that view, in the ninth book of the *De Augmentis*,
deserves, by its reverence and its noble form, to
stand beside Hooker's. Reason and conscience, he
says, suffice only to turn man away from vice ; they
cannot teach him his full duty, they cannot arrive at
the highest laws of conduct ; " ' Love your enemies '
does not sound human ; it is a voice beyond." Where
philosophy ends religion begins. Religion should welcome all increase of natural knowledge, because it leads
to the greater glory of God, and because it is a help
against unbelief. " A little philosophy inclineth the
mind to Atheism, but a further proceeding bringeth it
back to Religion."

CHAPTER VI

NEW ATLANTIS—HISTORICAL WORK—ESSAYS—STYLE

FROM Plato to Mr. H. G. Wells, reformers and dreamers
have been attracted by the plan of painting an ideal
State, in which their reforms are achieved and their
dreams fulfilled. Such a sketch of his ideal State
Bacon intended to give in the *New Atlantis*. He
completed only the account of what seemed to him its
most important institution—an ideal college of scientific research. To quote from Rawley's preface to the
first edition : " This fable my Lord devised to the end
that he might exhibit therein a model or description
of a College instituted for the interpreting of nature
and the producing of great and marvellous works for

the benefit of men. . . . His Lordship thought also in this present fable, to have composed a frame of laws, or of the best state or mould of a commonwealth : but foreseeing it would be a long work, his desire of collecting the natural history diverted him, which he preferred many degrees before it."

The interest of the *New Atlantis* is twofold : it furnishes a commentary on Bacon's philosophic aims, and it illustrates his magnificent powers of imagination and expression. From the first standpoint it adds new evidence of his desire to serve mankind, and of his faith in knowledge as the means ; it shows how that desire and that faith gave him the highest motives to seek " some honourable office in the State," so that, in his own words, " I might thus secure helps and supports to aid my labours, with a view to the accomplishment of my destined task." In some private notes made in July 1608, following remarks on the need for complete records of certain natural phenomena, he makes a list of various places of which he might aim at the headship, " to command wits and pens "— " Westminster, Eton, Winchester, specially Trinity College in Cambridge, St. John's in Cambridge, Maudlin College in Oxford." Then he notes the main heads of a scheme for a " College of Inventors." Some of the same ideas had already found expression in the *Praise of Knowledge*, and they occur again in the *Advancement.* Naturally Bacon's mind, with its strong instinct for the practical application of ideas, must have turned constantly from criticism of the defects of existing knowledge and of existing places of learning, and from the elaboration of the new method, to consider the possibility of practical reform by the foundation of a properly planned and properly conducted institution for research. The *New Atlantis* contains, in the account of " Solomon's House," the fullest and most mature expression of Bacon's conception of such a college. Some persons dream of a house they have never seen, until every detail is clear and real to them. For thirty years Bacon had dreamed day-dreams of a perfect home of learning, ex-

ploring its halls and gardens, its laboratories and libraries,
its towers and subterranean cells, until every detail lived
in his imagination.   So at the end he did not need
laboriously to plan his college before the reader's eyes ;
he had only to describe what he knew so well.   In
his packed yet lucid description he gives the impression of a guide striving to show as much as he can
in a brief time, selecting and summarizing, able to
indicate only his chief treasures.   We fall into the
rôle of the visitor ; in the "Father of Solomon's
House " magnificent in array, with " an aspect as if
he pitied men," we recognize Bacon ; in his sonorous
periods we hear Bacon speak : " First I will set forth
unto you the end of our foundation.   Secondly, the
preparations and instruments we have for our works.
Thirdly, the several employments and functions whereto
our Fellows are assigned.   And fourthly, the ordinances
and rites which we observe.

   " The end of our foundation is the knowledge of causes,
and secret motions of things ; and the enlarging of the
bounds of human nature, to the effecting of all things
possible."

   The " preparations and instruments " include facili-
ties for every kind of experiment.   Among the most
interesting of the discoveries prophesied here under the
form of description are the culture of " new plants
differing from the vulgar " ; surgical discoveries (by
vivisection of birds and beasts) such as the possibility
of removing certain organs formerly considered vital,
without causing death ; " glasses and means to see
small and minute bodies perfectly and distinctly ;
instruments to represent and imitate all articulate
sounds and letters, and the voices and notes of beasts
and birds " ; " means to convey sounds in trunks and
pipes, in strange lines, and distances " ; artificial scents
and flavours ; " degrees of flying in the air " ; " ships
and boats for going under water."   So shrewd are most
of Bacon's forecasts that we receive a distinct shock
when amongst them we find the old dream of a device
for perpetual motion.

NEW ATLANTIS 79

The labours of the thirty-six " Fellows " are elaborately organized. Twelve travel and bring back records
of research throughout the world ; these are called
" Merchants of Light." Three collect experiments
already on record. Three collect experiments " of all
Mechanical Arts and also of Liberal Sciences," and of
" practices " not recognized as scientific. Three tabu-
late the results of the workers already named. Three
devote themselves to the application of the experiments
of their fellows, " to draw out of them things of use,
and practice for Man's life, and knowledge." Three,
after consultation with all their fellow workers, plan
new experiments to develop the work already done,
as recommended in the *Novum Organum.* Three carry
out these experiments. Three perform the crowning
duty laid down for the philosopher in the *Novum
Organum* : working on the results of all the others,
they complete the highest steps of the inductive process, and establish the general principles. These are
called the " Interpreters of Nature."

" Two very long and fair galleries " form the museum
of the college, one filled with " patterns and samples of
all manner of the more rare and excellent inventions " ;
the other with statues " of all principal inventors."
Hymns and services are prescribed for daily praise and
prayer to God. Finally, arrangements are made for
the publication of all inventions as the College thinks
it expedient to popularize (some are kept secret) ; and
for issuing warnings and advice in matters of public
danger.

Harvey sneered that Bacon " writes philosophy like a
Lord Chancellor." The sneer may be turned to a just
compliment on the scheme of Solomon's House. Wisdom, shrewd practical insight, faculty for organization,
zeal for knowledge for its own sake and for the public
welfare, combine in this admirable manifesto of academic statesmanship. The founders of the London
" College of Philosophy," which in 1662 became the
Royal Society, acknowledged that they drew their
inspiration from Bacon's " Solomon's House " ; and

through three centuries science has slowly laboured to realize, in Universities and Technical Schools, a part of Bacon's programme. In academic administration, as in scientific method, he pointed the way.

The account of Solomon's House comes at the end of the fragment; the earlier part tells of the accidental arrival of the storm-driven and distressed ship's crew at the island called Bensalem, of their reception, and of the customs of the island. Here purpose is entirely subordinated to vivid fiction. Bacon intended to proceed, after the manner of More's Utopia, to a detailed account of the institutions and customs of the island, serving as an exposition of his own views. Of this, apart from the account of Solomon's House, only a few incidental passages were written. We learn that natives, except the Fellows of Solomon's House, are not allowed to travel abroad. Strangers, who appear seldom, are permitted access under certain restrictions, are treated most humanely, and are encouraged to settle. (Bacon shared the contempt expressed by so many Elizabethans for the travelled jackanapes who dressed his native folly in exaggerated imitation of French and Italian custom; but he felt the benefit which the best men could gain for themselves and their country from contact with other nations, and recognized the practical advantage to be gained from carefully supervised immigration.) To strengthen the bonds of large families a family conclave is customary, which receives both legal and religious sanction, and has an elaborate symbolical ceremonial. The people are particularly law-abiding and orderly; the rulers wise and benevolent. Officers and servants refuse to accept gifts from the guests : " When we offered him [a Notary] some Pistoletts, he smiling said : he must not be twice paid for one labour : meaning (as I take it) that he had salary sufficient of the State for his service." On the other hand, the Father of Solomon's House " assigned a value of about two thousand ducats, for a bounty to me and my fellows. For they give great largesses, where they come, upon all occasions." Here Bacon's own instinct for magnificence speaks, as in the account of the gorgeous garb and appointments of the " Father " and his retinue, and of other personages.

These particulars are interesting and illuminating, and we lament that more were not added ; but it would have been a greater loss if the introduction, where purpose plays the merest occasional part, had been omitted. Bacon's fictitious description produces the impression of reality more powerfully than that of any other writer before Defoe. He has Defoe's trick of giving exact unessential detail, and so suggesting the careful record of an eyewitness. The fragment opens as though summarized from a ship's log.[1] " Wee sayled from Peru, (wher wee had continued by the space of one whole yeare,) for China and Japan, by the South Sea ; taking with us Victuals for twelve Moneths ; And had good Windes from the east, though soft and weake, for five Moneths space, and more. But then the Winde came about, and setled in the west for many dayes, so that we could make little or no way, and were sometimes in purpose to move back. But then againe there arose Strong and Great Windes from the South, with a Point East ; which carried us up, (for all that we could doe) towards the north ; by which time our Victualls failed us, though we had made good spare of them. So that finding our selves, in the Midst of the greatest Wildernesse of Waters in the World, without Victuall, we gave ourselves up for lost Men, and prepared for Death."

All the circumstance and ceremonial of the family festival, mentioned above, are described with similar elaborate detail. It is even noted that the ivy which canopies the father's chair is " somewhat whiter than ours, like the leaf of a Silver Aspen but more shining." A final example may be taken from the description of the first communication between the ship and the natives. " Ther made forth to us a small Boate, with about eight Persons in it ; wherof One of them had in

[1] In this and the following extract I have preserved the spelling of the original edition, as the realism of the description would suffer by the jar between new spelling and old phrase.

his Hand a Tipstaffe of a yellow Cane, tipped at both
ends with Blew, who came aboard our Shipp, without
any shew of Distrust at all. . . . He drew forth a little
Scroule of Parchment, (somewhat yellower then our
Parchment, and shining like the Leaves of Writing
Tables, but otherwise soft and flexible,) and delivered
it to our foremost Man. . . . This Scroule was Signed
with a Stampe of Cherubins Wings, not spred, but
hanging downwarde ; And by them a Crosse."

The spirit of Bacon's work in natural philosophy
informs also his historical work. Fidelity to fact, careful progress from the fact to its explanation, and a
wide and clear view of his material as a connected
whole, mark his method. His strong royalist feeling
and his particular desire to please James I. make him
paint the character of Henry VII. in as favourable
colours as possible, but even here he is as impartial
as any English historian before the eighteenth century.
In grasp of the organic quality of history he again leads
the way. History is for him a department of philosophy ; he does not merely catalogue events, he shows
their connection and their significance.

Of Bacon's legal works and of his minor non-philo-
sophical works it need only be said that they illustrate
in their several departments the same qualities which
Bacon displayed in his practical activities ; those of
a strong mind, intensely though impersonally benevolent, concentrated on actual facts : zeal for reform and
wisdom in directing it, tempered to compromise by
respect for the established order ; an unfailing and
unrelaxing grip of the essential, an admirable power of
organized statement.

From Bacon's own day, the most popular of his
writings have been the Essays ; and this is natural,
for they claim as audience not merely the limited circle
to whom his philosophical, professional and political
works appeal, but all who are interested to know the
mature opinion of a great-minded man of the world
on the problems and circumstances of everyday life.
Six editions appeared in Bacon's lifetime ; the first in

1597, including only ten essays, bound up with the *Sacred Meditations* and *Colours of Good and Evil;* reprints of the whole volume in 1598, 1604, and 1606; a new edition of the essays alone in 1612, omitting the essay "Of Honour and Reputation," correcting and enlarging the other nine (Of Studie, Discourse, Ceremonies and Respects, Followers and Friends, Suitors, Expense, Regiment of Health, Faction, Negociating), and adding twenty-nine new essays;[1] and in 1625 the final edition of fifty-eight essays, on which the modern texts are based, including the thirty-eight of the 1612 edition, in most cases revised and enlarged, a revised and enlarged version of the essay "Of Honour and Reputation," and nineteen new essays.

The title "Essays" (probably borrowed from Montaigne, whose *Essais* had appeared in 1580) indicates Bacon's purpose. They are expressions of personal opinion to weigh or test its truth, without attempt at proof; as distinct from the exactly based and scientifically demonstrated statements of his philosophical work, and from the records of facts and of thoughts preliminary thereto. The subject-matter changes with the growth of his personal interests and experience. He writes in the first ten essays on everyday subjects attractive to the student of men and affairs. Of the essays added in 1612 some extend the range of political subjects from the wider experience of the mature statesman (*e.g.*, Of Great Place of Empire, Of Judicature, Of Greatness of Kingdoms). Others analyse human motives, consider the problems of individual relationship and conduct, and weigh the ultimate values of life (*e.g.*, Of Marriage and Single Life, Of Parents and Children, Of Young Men and Age, Of Friendship, Of Love, Of Seeming Wise, Of Ambition, Of Fortune, Of Atheism, Of Religion, Of Death). The final edition extends both groups, adding to the former such subjects as Plantations, Seditions and Troubles; to the latter, with

---

[1] The table of contents names *forty* essays; but the last two ("Of the Publike" and "Of Warre and Peace") are not given in this or any other edition.

sad significance, Revenge, Anger, Envy, Adversity, the Vicissitudes of Things. One little group of the latest essays, however, opens up new ground. He writes " Of Masks and Triumphs "—apologetically, for " these things are but toyes to come among such serious observations," but still with a definiteness of opinion on arrangement and staging that betrays relish and reminds us that he wrote "devices" for Essex. Still more pleasantly, he turns to his own hobbies in the essays " Of Building " and " Of Gardens." His opening advice on building illustrates his practical sense : " Houses are built to live in, and not to look on ; therefore let use be preferred before uniformity [*i.e.* symmetrical beauty] except where both may be had." Later in the essay, however, he gives play to the desire for richness which characterized his work on his own house at Gorhambury. But while he was interested in buildings, he loved gardens : " God Almighty first planted a garden. And indeed it is the purest of human pleasures. It is the greatest refreshment to the spirit of man." Even his technical directions, such as those for a sequence of flowers all the year round, read poetically ; and his list of sweet-scented flowers carries all the fragrance of an English garden. " And because the breath of flowers is far sweeter in the air (where it comes and goes, like the warbling of music) than in the hand, therefore nothing is more fit for that delight than to know what be the flowers and plants that do best perfume the air. . . . Sweetbriar. Then wallflowers, which are very delightful to be set under a parlour or lower chamber window, then pinks and gillyflowers, specially the matted pink and clove gillyflower." His garden would be a little formal for a romantic taste, but he despises the extremes of formality ; the hedges must not be " too busy or full of work. . . . I do not like images cut out in Juniper or other garden stuff ; they be for children " ; while " as for the making of knots or figures with divers coloured earths, . . . they be but toys : you may see as good sights, many times, in tarts." He gives up a third of his desired thirty acres (for it is the " prince-

like " garden he describes) to lawn ; and another third
to a heath, " framed, as much as may be, to a natural
wildness," with thickets " of sweetbriar and honey-
suckle, and some wild-vine amongst ; and the ground
set with violets, strawberries and primroses. For these
are sweet and prosper in the shade. And these to be
in the heath, here and there, not in any order." And
on the little hillocks must grow wild thyme and
germander, periwinkle and violets, strawberries, pinks,
cowslips, daisies, and other plants "sweet and
sightly."

Bacon's garden was only for occasional delight, and
for retirement ; his life belonged to the law courts, to
Parliament, to Whitehall, or in its times of freedom
from such duties, to his study. The best fruit of his
serious thought was stored in his philosophical work.
In the essays, it is the man of the world rather than
the philosopher who speaks. Wherever strong and alert
common sense can serve, Bacon is admirable ; wherever
remoter speculation is needed, he falls short ; wherever
emotion is needed, he fails utterly. In writing of motives
and duties his nobler ideals stand out clearly, but he
lacks faith in them ; he has learnt from Machiavelli
and from experience to see men's weaknesses, and he
cannot trust the strength of simple goodness. Goodness is " the greatest of all virtues and dignities of the
mind, being the character of the deity, and without it
man is a busy, mischievous, wretched thing, no better
than a kind of vermin." Yet it is the cross-grained,
malignant men, he says, who make the best politicians.
He does not make such observations sadly, or with
conscious cynicism ; he merely states the fact, a little
bitterly if he has suffered, but even then without moral
indignation. So with many of his observations.
" There is in human nature generally more of the fool
than of the wise ; and therefore those faculties by
which the foolish part of men's minds is taken are most
potent." " The wiser sort of great persons bring in ever
upon the stage somebody upon whom to derive [divert]
the envy that would come upon themselves." " There is

rarely any rising, but by a commixture of good and evil arts."

The general tendency of his remarks on conduct is, Be wary ; gain trust, but give it only most cautiously ; foster your own virtues, but do not expect them in others ; aim at great ends, and to compass them use the weaknesses of human nature. With this spirit, un-corrected by the insight of emotion, it is natural that his reflections on friendship and love, on the relation of husband and wife, of parent and child, are shallow and cheap. His glance rests shrewdly enough on the external and practical aspects, and he expresses his superficial judgments in phrases at once so picturesque and so terse that their commonplaces strike like dis-coveries. " He that hath wife and children hath given hostages to fortune ; for they are impediments to great enterprises, either of virtue or mischief. . . . The most ordinary cause of a single life is liberty ; especially in certain self-pleasing and humorous minds, which are so sensible of every restraint as they will go near to think their girdles and garters to be bonds and shackles. . . . A single life doth well with Churchmen ; for Charity will hardly water the ground, where it must first fill a pool."

Every word tells ; yet how little and pitiful it all seems in comparison with any great idealist's utterance. Compare, for example, the last sentence quoted with Shelley's repeated declaration that love grows as it gives. " True love in this differs from gold and clay— that to divide is not to take away." In the essay " Of Love " Bacon spends all but the last two sentences on the follies of love. " The stage is more beholding to love than the life of man. For as to the stage, love is ever a matter of comedies, and now and then of tragedies : but in life it doth much mischief, sometimes like a siren, sometimes like a fury. . . . They do best who, if they cannot but admit love, yet sever it wholly from their serious affairs and actions of life." Between man and woman, Bacon thinks only of passion divorced from deeper love. He cannot, like Sidney and Shakespeare, find even in passion something of the infinite and eternal ; still less can he comprehend its service of the spiritual, or conceive that love may be the finest flower of friendship, blossoming perfectly because rooted in every human longing, religious in its revelation of spirit incarnate. The marriage service of his prayer-book might have served as his text. His judgment corresponds to his experience. He never loved a woman ; he married for convenience, covering with gorgeous ceremonial trappings the drab commonplace of a business arrangement ; he never devotedly loved relation or friend.

Bacon sets friendship higher than love, and treats it less inadequately. He speaks wisely of the mutual usefulness of friends, and of the stimulus to thought given by friendly conversation ; but the nearest approach to a sense of something higher in friendship than mutual service comes in the recognition that man instinctively craves friendship. "A crowd is not company ; and faces are but a gallery of pictures ; and talk but a tinkling cymbal where there is no love. . . . It is a mere and miserable solitude to want true friends, without which the world is but a wilderness." This rises above the utilitarian view prominent in the essay ; but even here there is no glimmer of the flame that burns in Shakespeare's sonnets.

The same limitations mark the essays touching metaphysical subjects. "*What is truth?* said jesting Pilate ; and would not stay for an answer," begins the essay " Of Truth." Bacon himself does not furnish an answer. He speaks eloquently about truth, but he never inquires into its essential nature. In the essay " Of Atheism," he states his view that knowledge and experience alike support religion, and incidentally he makes some acute observations—*e.g.* " All that impugn a received religion, or superstition, are by the adverse part, branded with the name of atheist." But he notices only the immediate causes of atheism—the first tincture of philosophy, divisions in religion, and so on ; he does not try to grasp the condition of the mind which would willingly believe but cannot. His own religious belief is sincere and definite, but its definiteness comes, not from clear answers to fundamental questions, but from absence of the desire to question. His eager and inquisitive spirit sets bounds to its inquiries, and never passes beyond subjects where the senses can perceive facts and the intellect prove principles, to speculate on the unprovable. He never shows any inclination towards speculation. His recognition of the limits of the intellect springs not from the instinct to believe, like Sir Thomas Browne's, not from reasoned argument, like Hooker's, but from the indifference of his imagination to metaphysical problems, confirmed by a sense of the futility of earlier metaphysical speculation. He writes " Of Death " without any hint of meditation about the future life ; rather in the temper of Marcus Aurelius than of a Christian. The essay is only some six hundred words long ; it includes no less than eleven classical illustrations ; its only debt to Christianity lies in two phrases. An example may show the admirable vigour and strong sense of the essay, and at the same time its narrow range. " Men fear Death, as children fear to go in the dark : and as that natural fear in children is increased with tales, so is the other. . . . Groans and convulsions, and a discoloured face, and friends weeping, and blacks, and obsequies, and the like, shew Death terrible. It is worthy the observing, that there is no passion in the mind of man so weak, but it mates and masters the fear of Death ; and therefore Death is no such terrible enemy, when a man hath so many attendants about him that can win the combat of him. Revenge triumphs over Death ; Love slights it ; Honour aspireth to it ; Grief flieth to it. . . . It is as natural to die as to be born ; and to a little infant, perhaps, the one is as painful as the other."

Similarly in the essays discussing ethical problems, and the circumstances in life of which Christian teaching has most definitely treated, Bacon's avowed religious beliefs remain strangely aloof. It would scarcely seem possible to write of revenge without a thought

of the New Testament; but Bacon does this, choosing
his illustrations from the Old Testament, and from
classical and Renascence history. He passes by the
ethical problem, and considers only the social bearing
and the personal result of revenge. Similarly in the essay
"Of Adversity," despite reference to both Testaments,
the opening quotation from Seneca strikes the keynote;
the essay praises fortitude, not meek resignation; the
tone is that of Boethius, not that of the Gospels or even
of the Psalms.

Even the brief quotations already given, from essays
where the subject is not the most apt to Bacon's treatment, show his acute observation, his massive common
sense, his vivid and pithy style. These qualities shine
still more brightly in the essays on political subjects,
and on the general habits, characters and circumstances of men, where the matter is covered by Bacon's
experience and suited to his method of treatment.
The wisdom and insight, the shrewd realization of
existing conditions, the unmoved recognition and occasional exploitation of men's weaknesses, which marked
Bacon's State papers, inspire the essays on questions
of State policy (*e.g.* Of Unity in Religion, Of Seditions
and Troubles, Of Empire, Of Innovations, Of the True
Greatness of Kingdoms, Of Plantations). The sturdy
independence of tradition manifested at every step of
his philosophical work, informs his opinions " Of Custom
and Education." But most noteworthy of all are the
essays on men's characters and customs. They are
packed with acute observation strikingly expressed.
They paint human nature and human activities, not
as seen by the poet, " by lightning flashes," but as seen
by the philosophical politician, by the "daylight of
truth," by the brightest light of common day.

" We take Cunning for a sinister or crooked wisdom.
And certainly, there is great difference between a
cunning man and a wise man, not only in point of
honesty, but in point of ability. There be that can
pack the cards, and yet cannot play well; so there are
some that are good in canvasses and factions, that are

otherwise weak men. . . . These cunning men are
like haberdashers of small wares." (*Of Cunning*.)

" Affected dispatch is one of the most dangerous
things to business that can be. . . . Measure not dispatch by the times of sitting, but by the advancement
of the business. . . . I knew a wise man that had it
for a byword, when he saw men hasten to a conclusion,
' Stay a little, that we may make an end the sooner.' "
(*Of Dispatch*.)

" Suspicions amongst thoughts are like bats amongst
birds ; they ever fly by twilight." (*Of Suspicion*.)

" He that hath a satirical vein, as he maketh others
afraid of his wit, so he had need be afraid of others'
memory. He that questioneth much shall learn much
and content much ; but especially if he apply his
questions to the skill of the persons whom he asketh ;
for he shall give them occasion to please themselves
in speaking, and himself shall continually gather knowledge. But let his questions not be troublesome ;
for that is fit for a poser [examiner]. And let him be
sure to leave other men their turns to speak. . . . Dis-
cretion of speech is more than eloquence ; and to
speak agreeably to him, with whom we deal, is more
than to speak in good words or in good order." (*Of
Discourse*.)

" As the baggage is to an army, so is riches to virtue.
It cannot be spared nor left behind, but it hindereth
the march ; yea, and the care of it, sometimes, loseth
or disturbeth the victory." (*Of Riches*.)

" Money is like muck, not good except it be spread."
(*Of Seditions and Troubles*.)

" Read not to contradict and confute ; nor to
believe and take for granted ; nor to find talk and
discourse ; but to weigh and consider. Some books are
to be tasted, others to be swallowed, and some few to be
chewed and digested. . . . Reading maketh a full man ;
conference [conversation] a ready man ; and writing
an exact man." (*Of Studies*.)

" Men's behaviour should be like their apparel, not
too strait or point device [stiff or punctilious], but

free for exercise **or** motion." (*Of Ceremonies and Respects.*)

A pioneer in so many directions, Bacon nevertheless lagged behind his age in one respect. He distrusted his own language. From the very beginnings of the Renascence, catholic love of beauty, embracing the modern as well as the ancient, and strong sense of nationality had combined to give each "noble vulgar tongue" its due glory, even with those who most admired the classics. Dante and Castiglione, Ronsard and Du Bellay, Sir Thomas More and Ascham, had formally defended the vernaculars, while the further examples of Ariosto and Rabelais, of Spenser and Shakespeare, of Wyclif and Hooker, had proved indisputably the adequacy of modern languages to most various tasks. Yet Bacon, rebel though he was to the authority of classical thought, clung to Latin as the only medium for work destined " to the next age and foreign nations." There is no matter for surprise in his preference for the international tongue of learning; but he was strangely unjust to his own language, which he used so admirably. " These modern languages will at one time or another play the bankrupt with books," he wrote to Toby Matthew; and again, on the appearance of the *De Augmentis*, he declared " It is a book that will live and be a citizen of the world, as English books are not." He wrote his most important work, the *Novum Organum*, as well as many minor works, in Latin; and all that he valued highly in his English work he either translated or caused to be translated into Latin.

Scarcely less unpromising for Bacon's style sounds his condemnation of the attention paid to form in writing by the schoolmen; but here his attack was levelled against the poverty of the matter so elaborately enshrined, rather than against care for style. His own style, both as orator and writer, was the result of an art perfect enough to conceal its labour. His commonplace books show how carefully he prepared his effects: he collected similes, metaphors, quotations, allusions, for every connection; he noted the effect of apparent carelessness and abruptness as well as of the commoner rhetorical devices. Speaking and writing to convince his countrymen more often than merely to record his views, he was obliged to use English, and to labour for effective form. Above all, his lucidity and vigour of thought, and his imaginative power, as fertile intellectually as it was barren emotionally, informed his style; and he wrought magnificently with the tool he despised.

Bacon was master of two styles. In the essays, especially in the earliest draft, he aims at and achieves the utmost vigour of terse speech. The sentences fall like hammer-blows. Ben Jonson, whose prose comes nearest to Bacon's in this respect, may well have had his style in mind when he wrote "a strict and succinct style is that where you can take away nothing without loss, and that loss to be manifest." Bacon's terseness does not mean bareness. The essays sparkle with brilliant imagery and apt allusion and quotation; but these are no mere surface ornaments: they are built into the structure, strengthening it while they decorate it. Nor does this fine economy mean obscurity. The only source of obscurity in Bacon's style lies in his occasional Latinisms, and it must be remembered that these would not cause difficulty to his readers in an age when Latin was the basis of all education. The short sentences of the earlier essays produce a certain staccato effect, but their style cannot justly be called jerky. Each sentence is a well squared block, and the whole essay is built firmly without need of the mortar of connectives.

In the later essays the style varies between this packed brevity and the more elaborately organized style of the English philosophical works, the historical works and the *New Atlantis*. In the philosophical works above all, Bacon shows himself master of a stately and sonorous English; and the picturesque and vivid illustrations which sparkle in the clean-cut brevity of his epigrammatic style grow, in more spacious work, into a wealth of glowing colour. But even here order and economy reign among the heaped treasures of imaginative eloquence. Ben Jonson's tribute to his oratory may be applied to his written work. " No man ever spake more neatly, more pressedly, more weightily, or suffered less emptiness, less idleness, in what he uttered. No member of his speech but consisted of his own graces. His hearers could not cough, or look aside from him without loss. He commanded where he spoke, and had his judges angry and pleased at his devotion. No man had their affections more in his power. The fear of every man that heard him was lest he should make an end."

In Bacon's greatness as an orator lies the secret of his characteristic greatness as a writer. All his work directly addresses an audience. Read aloud any passage from the English philosophical works, and you hear the splendid and sonorous harmonies of great speech ; read aloud the essays, and you hear the rattle and crack of quick debate. Hooker's best prose is even more musical, Sir Thomas Browne's richer alike in music and colour, Milton's vaster in its overwhelming might ; but no writer of prose before Burke equals Bacon in the sustained persuasive combination of lucidity and beauty.

CHRONOLOGICAL SUMMARY AND INDEX

BIOGRAPHY

CHIEF WORKS